Lecture Notes in Artificial Intelligence 11985

Subseries of Lecture Notes in Computer Science

More information about this series at http://www.springer.com/series/1244

Valerio Bitetta · Ilaria Bordino ·
Andrea Ferretti · Francesco Gullo ·
Stefano Pascolutti · Giovanni Ponti (Eds.)

Mining Data for Financial Applications

4th ECML PKDD Workshop, MIDAS 2019
Würzburg, Germany, September 16, 2019
Revised Selected Papers

 Springer

Editors
Valerio Bitetta
UniCredit
Milan, Italy

Ilaria Bordino
UniCredit
Rome, Italy

Andrea Ferretti
UniCredit
Milan, Italy

Francesco Gullo
UniCredit
Rome, Italy

Stefano Pascolutti
UniCredit
Milan, Italy

Giovanni Ponti
ENEA Portici Research Center
Portici, Italy

ISSN 0302-9743　　　　　　ISSN 1611-3349　(electronic)
Lecture Notes in Artificial Intelligence
ISBN 978-3-030-37719-9　　　ISBN 978-3-030-37720-5　(eBook)
https://doi.org/10.1007/978-3-030-37720-5

LNCS Sublibrary: SL7 – Artificial Intelligence

This Springer imprint is published by the registered company Springer Nature Switzerland AG
The registered company address is: Gewerbestrasse 11, 6330 Cham, Switzerland

Preface

MIDAS 2019: The 4th Workshop on MIning DAta for financial applicationS

Workshop Description

Motivation. Like the famous King Midas, popularly remembered in Greek mythology for his ability to turn everything he touched with his hands into gold, the wealth of data generated by modern technologies, with widespread presence of computers, users, and media connected by Internet, is a goldmine for tackling a variety of problems in the financial domain.

Nowadays, people's interactions with technological systems provide us with gargantuan amounts of data documenting collective behavior in a previously unimaginable fashion. Recent research has shown that by properly modeling and analyzing these massive datasets, for instance representing them as network structures, it is possible to gain useful insights into the evolution of the systems considered (i.e., trading, disease spreading, political elections). Investigating the impact of data arising from today's application domains on financial decisions is of paramount importance. Knowledge extracted from data can help gather critical information for trading decisions, reveal early signs of impactful events (such as stock market moves), or anticipate catastrophic events (e.g., financial crises) that result from a combination of actions, and affect humans worldwide.

The importance of data-mining tasks in the financial domain has been long recognized. For example, in the Web context, changes in the frequency with which users browse news or look for certain terms on search engines have been correlated with product trends, level of activity in certain given industries, unemployment rates, or car and home sales, as well as stock-market trade volumes and price movements. Other core applications include forecasting the stock market, predicting bank bankruptcies, understanding and managing financial risk, trading futures, credit rating, loan management, bank customer profiling. Despite its well-recognized relevance and some recent related efforts, data mining in finance is still not stably part of the main stream of data-mining conferences. This makes the topic particularly appealing for a workshop proposal, whose small, interactive, and possibly interdisciplinary context provides a unique opportunity to advance research in a stimulating but still quite unexplored field.

Objectives and Topics. The aim of the 4th Workshop on MIning DAta for financial applicationS (MIDAS 2019), held in conjunction with the 2019 European Conference on Machine Learning and Principles and Practice of Knowledge Discovery in Databases (ECML-PKDD 2019), Würzburg, Germany, September 16–20, 2019, was to discuss challenges, potentialities, and applications of leveraging data-mining tasks to tackle problems in the financial domain. The workshop provided a premier forum for sharing findings, knowledge, insights, experience and lessons learned from mining data generated in various domains. The intrinsic interdisciplinary nature of the workshop promoted the interaction between computer scientists, physicists, mathematicians, economists, and financial analysts, thus paving the way for an exciting and stimulating environment involving researchers and practitioners from different areas.

Topics of interest included: forecasting the stock market, trading models, discovering market trends, predictive analytics for financial services, network analytics in finance, planning investment strategies, portfolio management, understanding and managing financial risk, customer/investor profiling, identifying expert investors, financial modeling, measures of success in forecasting, anomaly detection in financial data, fraud detection, discovering patterns and correlations in financial data, text mining and NLP for financial applications, financial network analysis, time series analysis, and pitfall identification.

Outcomes. MIDAS 2019 was structured as a full-day workshop. We encouraged submissions of regular papers (long or short), and extended abstracts. Regular papers could be up to 15 pages (long papers) or 8 pages (short papers), and reported on novel, unpublished work that might not be mature enough for a conference or journal submission. Extended abstracts could be up to five pages long, and presented work-in-progress, recently published work fitting the workshop topics, or position papers. All submitted papers were peer-reviewed by three reviewers from the Program Committee, and selected on the basis of these reviews. MIDAS 2019 received 16 submissions, among which 11 papers were accepted (8 long papers and 3 short papers).

In accordance with the reviewers' scores and comments, the paper entitled "Curriculum Learning in Deep Neural Networks for Financial Forecasting" authored by Allison Koenecke and Amita Gajewar, was selected as the best paper of the workshop. The paper entitled "MQLV: Optimal Policy of Money Management in Retail Banking with Q-Learning" authored by Jeremy Charlier, Gaston Ormazabal, Radu State, and Jean Hilger, was recognized as runner up.

The program of the workshop was enriched by an invited speaker: Dr. Marcello Paris from UniCredit, R&D Department, who gave a talk titled "Homology-based Learning: Shapes for Financial Time Series."

June 2019

Valerio Bitetta
Ilaria Bordino
Andrea Ferretti
Francesco Gullo
Stefano Pascolutti
Giovanni Ponti

Organization

Program Chairs

Valerio Bitetta	UniCredit, Italy
Ilaria Bordino	UniCredit, Italy
Andrea Ferretti	UniCredit, Italy
Francesco Gullo	UniCredit, Italy
Stefano Pascolutti	UniCredit, Italy
Giovanni Ponti	ENEA, Italy

Program Committee

Aris Anagnostopoulos	Sapienza University, Italy
Argimiro Arratia	Universitat Politécnica de Catalunya, Spain
Antonia Azzini	C2T, Italy
Xiao Bai	Yahoo Research, USA
Luca Barbaglia	JRC - European Commission, Italy
Ludovico Boratto	Eurecat, Spain
Cristian Bravo	University of Southampton, UK
Doug Burdick	IBM Research, USA
Alejandra Cabaña	Universitat Autónoma de Barcelona, Spain
Annalina Caputo	Trinity College Dublin, Ireland
Sergio Consoli	JRC - European Commission, Italy
Carlotta Domeniconi	George Mason University, USA
Wouter Duivesteijn	Eindhoven University of Technology, The Netherlands
Roberto Interdonato	CIRAD, France
Andreas Kaltenbrunner	NTENT, Spain
Dragi Kocev	Jožef Stefan Institute, Slovenia
Nicolas Kourtellis	Telefonica Research, Spain
Iordanis Koutsopoulos	Athens University of Economics and Business, Greece
Ralf Krestel	Hasso Plattner Institute, Germany
Rajasekar Krishnamurthy	University of Massachusetts Amherst, USA
Elisa Letizia	European Central Bank, Germany
Matteo Manca	Zurich Insurance, Switzerland
Stefania Marrara	C2T, Italy
Yelena Mejova	ISI Foundation, Italy
Davide Mottin	Aarhus University, Denmark
Luca Rossini	Vrije Universiteit Amsterdam, The Netherlands
Carlos Sarraute	Grandata Labs, Spain
Tatevik Sekhposyan	Texas A&M University, USA
Letizia Tanca	Politecnico of Milan, Italy
Turki Turki	New Jersey Institute of Technology, USA

Ali Caner Turkmen   Boğaziçi University, Turkey
Antti Ukkonen   University of Helsinki, Finland
Edoardo Vacchi   Red Hat, Italy
George Valkanas   Detectica, USA

Contents

MQLV: Optimal Policy of Money Management in Retail Banking with Q-Learning

Jeremy Charlier[1,2], Gaston Ormazabal[2(✉)], Radu State[1], and Jean Hilger[3]

[1] University of Luxembourg, 1855 Luxembourg, Luxembourg
{jeremy.charlier,radu.state}@uni.lu
[2] Columbia University, New York, NY 10027, USA
{jjc2292,gso7}@columbia.edu
[3] BCEE, 1160 Luxembourg, Luxembourg
j.hilger@bcee.lu

Abstract. Reinforcement learning has become one of the best approach to train a computer game emulator capable of human level performance. In a reinforcement learning approach, an optimal value function is learned across a set of actions, or decisions, that leads to a set of states giving different rewards, with the objective to maximize the overall reward. A policy assigns to each state-action pairs an expected return. We call an optimal policy a policy for which the value function is optimal. QLBS, Q-Learner in the Black-Scholes(-Merton) Worlds, applies the reinforcement learning concepts, and noticeably, the popular Q-learning algorithm, to the financial stochastic model of Black, Scholes and Merton. It is, however, specifically optimized for the geometric Brownian motion and the vanilla options. Its range of application is, therefore, limited to vanilla option pricing within the financial markets. We propose MQLV, Modified Q-Learner for the Vasicek model, a new reinforcement learning approach that determines the optimal policy of money management based on the aggregated financial transactions of the clients. It unlocks new frontiers to establish personalized credit card limits or bank loan applications, targeting the retail banking industry. MQLV extends the simulation to mean reverting stochastic diffusion processes and it uses a digital function, a Heaviside step function expressed in its discrete form, to estimate the probability of a future event such as a payment default. In our experiments, we first show the similarities between a set of historical financial transactions and Vasicek generated transactions and, then, we underline the potential of MQLV on generated Monte Carlo simulations. Finally, MQLV is the first Q-learning Vasicek-based methodology addressing transparent decision making processes in retail banking.

Keywords: Q-learning · Monte Carlo · Payment transactions

V. Bitetta et al. (Eds.): MIDAS 2019, LNAI 11985, pp. 1–15, 2020.
https://doi.org/10.1007/978-3-030-37720-5_1

1   Introduction

A major goal of the reinforcement learning (RL) and Machine Learning (ML) community is to build efficient representations of the current environment to solve complex tasks. In RL, an agent relies on multiple sensory inputs and past experience to derive a set of plausible actions to solve a new situation [1]. While the initial idea around RL is not new [2–4], significant progress has been achieved recently by combining neural networks and Deep Learning (DL) with RL. The progress of DL [5,6] has allowed the development of a novel agent combining RL with a class of deep artificial neural networks [1,7] resulting in Deep Q Network (DQN). The Q refers to the Q-learning algorithm introduced in [8]. It is an incremental method that successively improves its evaluations of the quality of the state-action pairs. The DQN approach achieves human level performance on Atari video games using unprocessed pixels as inputs. In [9], deep RL with double Q-Learning was proposed to challenge the DQN approach while trying to reduce the overestimation of the action values, a well-known drawback of the Q-learning and DQN methodologies. The extension of the DQN approach from discrete to continuous action domain, directly from the raw pixels to inputs, was successfully achieved for various simulated tasks [10].

Nonetheless, most of the proposed models focused on gaming theory and computer game simulation and very few to the financial world. In QLBS [11], a RL approach is applied to the Black, Scholes and Merton financial framework for derivatives [12,13], a cornerstone of the modern quantitative finance. In the BSM model, the dynamic of a stock market is defined as following a Geometric Brownian Motion (GBM) to estimate the price of a vanilla option on a stock [14]. A vanilla option is an option that gives the holder the right to buy or sell the underlying asset, a stock, at maturity for a certain price, the strike price. QLBS is one of the first approach to propose a complete RL framework for finance. As mentioned by the author, a certain number of topics are, however, not covered in the approach. For instance, it is specifically designed for vanilla options and it fails to address any other type of financial applications. Additionally, the initial generated paths rely on the popular GBM but there exist a significant number of other popular stochastic models depending on the market dynamics [15].

In this work, we describe a RL approach tailored for personal recommendation in retail banking regarding money management to be used for loan applications or credit card limits. The method is part of a banking strategy trying to reduce the customer churn in a context of a competitive retail banking market. We rely on the Q-learning algorithm and on a mean reverting diffusion process to address this topic. It leads ultimately to a fitted Q-iteration update and a model-free and off-policy setting. The diffusion process reflects the time series observed in retail banking such as transaction payments or credit card transactions. Such data is, however, strictly confidential and protected by the regulators, and therefore, it cannot be released publicly. Furthermore, we introduce a new terminal digital function, Π, defined as a Heaviside step function in its discrete form for a discrete variable $n \in \mathbb{R}$. The digital function is at the core of our approach for retail banking since it can evaluate the future probability of an event including, for instance, the future default probability of a client based on his spendings. Our method converges to an optimal policy, and to optimal sets of actions and states, respectively the spendings and the available money. The retail banks can, consequently, determine the optimal policy of money management based on the aggregated financial transactions of the clients. The banks are able to compare the difference between the MQLV's optimal policy and the individual policy of each client. It contributes to an unbiased decision making process while offering transparency to the client. Our main contributions are summarized below:

- A new RL framework called MQLV, Modified Q-Learning for Vasicek, extending the initial QLBS framework [11]. MQLV uses the theoretical foundation of RL learning and Q-Learning to build a financial RL framework based on a mean reverting diffusion process, the Vasicek model [16], to simulate data, in order to reach ultimately a model-free and off-policy RL setting.
- The definition of a digital function to estimate the future probability of an event. The aim is to widen the application perspectives of MQLV by using a characteristic terminal function that is usable for a decision making process in retail banking such as the estimation of the default probability of a client.
- The first application of Q-learning to determine the clients' optimal policy of money management in retail banking. MQLV leverages the clients aggregated financial transactions to define the optimal policy of money management, targeting the risk estimation of bank loan applications or credit cards.

The paper is structured as follows. In Sect. 2, we review QLBS and the Q-Learning formulations derived by Halperin in [11] in the context of the Black, Scholes and Merton model. In Sect. 3, we describe MQLV according to the Q-Learning algorithm that leads to a model-free and off-policy setting. We highlight experimental results in Sect. 4. We discuss related works in Sect. 5 and we conclude in Sect. 6 by addressing promising directions for future work.

2   Background

We define $A_t \in \mathcal{A}$ the action taken at time t for a given state $X_t \in \mathcal{X}$ and the immediate reward by R_{t+1}. The ongoing state is denoted by $X_t \in \mathcal{X}$ and the stochastic diffusion process by $S_t \in \mathcal{S}$ at time t. The discount factor that trades off the importance of immediate and later rewards is expressed by $\gamma \in [0; 1]$.

We recall a policy is a mapping from states to probabilities of selecting each possible action [17]. By following the notations of [11], the policy π such that

$$\pi : \{0, \dots, T-1\} \times \mathcal{X} \to \mathcal{A} \tag{1}$$

maps at time t the current state $X_t = x_t$ into the action $a_t \in \mathcal{A}$.

$$a_t = \pi(t, x_t) \tag{2}$$

The value of a state x under a policy π, denoted by $v_\pi(x)$ when starting in x and following π thereafter, is called the state-value function for policy π.

$$v_\pi = \mathbb{E}_\pi \left[\sum_{k=0}^{\infty} \gamma^k R_{t+k+1} | X_t = x \right] \tag{3}$$

The action-value function, $q_\pi(x, a)$ for policy π defines the value of taking action a in state x under a policy π as the expected return starting from x, taking the action a, and thereafter following policy π.

$$q_\pi(x, a) = \mathbb{E}_\pi \left[\sum_{k=0}^{\infty} \gamma^k R_{t+k+1} | X_t = x, A_t = a \right] \tag{4}$$

The optimal policy, π_t^*, is the policy that maximizes the state-value function.

$$\pi_t^*(X_t) = \arg \max_\pi V_t^\pi(X_t) \tag{5}$$

The optimal state-value function, V_t^*, satisfies the Bellman optimality equation such that

$$V_t^*(X_t) = \mathbb{E}_t^{\pi^*} \left[R_t(X_t, u_t = \pi_t^*(X_t), X_{t+1}) + \gamma V_{t+1}^*(X_{t+1}) \right]. \tag{6}$$

The Bellman equation for the action-value function, the Q-function, is defined as

$$Q_t^\pi(x, a) = \mathbb{E}_t \left[R_t(X_t, a_t, X_{t+1}) | X_t = x, a_t = a \right] + \gamma \mathbb{E}_t^\pi \left[V_{t+1}^\pi(X_{t+1}) | X_t = x \right]. \tag{7}$$

The optimal action-value function, Q_t^*, is obtained for the optimal policy with

$$\pi_t^* = \arg \max_\pi Q_t^\pi(x, a). \tag{8}$$

The optimal state-value and action-value functions are connected by the following system of equations.

$$\begin{cases} V_t^* = \max_a Q^*(x, a) \\ Q_t^* = \mathbb{E}_t \left[R_t(X_t, a, X_{t+1}) \right] + \gamma \mathbb{E}_t \left[V_{t+1}^*(X_{t+1} | X_t = x) \right] \end{cases} \tag{9}$$

Therefore, we can obtain the Bellman optimality equation.

$$Q_t^*(x, a) = \mathbb{E}_t \left[R_t(X_t, a_t, X_{t+1}) + \gamma \max_{a_{t+1} \in \mathcal{A}} Q_{t+1}^*(X_{t+1}, a_{t+1}) | X_t = x, a_t = a \right] \tag{10}$$

Using the Robbins-Monro update [18], the update rule for the optimal Q-function with on-line Q-learning on the data point $(X_t^{(n)}, a_t^{(n)}, R_t^{(n)}, X_{t+1}^{(n)})$ is expressed by the following equation with α a constant step-size parameter.

$$Q_t^{*,k+1}(X_t, a_t) = (1 - \alpha^k) Q_t^{*,k}(X_t, a_t)$$
$$+ \alpha^k \left[R_t(X_t, a_t, X_{t+1}) + \gamma \max_{a_{t+1} \in \mathcal{A}} Q_{t+1}^{*,k}(X_{t+1}, a_{t+1}) \right] \quad (11)$$

3 Algorithm

We describe, in this section, how to derive a general recursive formulation for the optimal action. It is equivalent to an optimal hedge under a financial framework such as, for instance, portfolio or personal finance optimization. We additionally present the formulation of the action-value function, the Q-function. Both the optimal hedge and the Q-function follow the assumption of a continuous space scenario generated by the Vasicek model with Monte Carlo simulation.

By relying on the financial framework established in [11], we consider a mean reverting diffusion process, also known as the Vasicek model [16].

$$dS_t = \kappa(b - S_t)dt + \sigma dB_t \quad (12)$$

The term κ is the speed reversion, b the long term mean level, σ the volatility and B_t the Brownian motion. The solution of the stochastic equation is equal to

$$S_t = S_0 e^{-\kappa t} + b(1 - e^{-\kappa t}) + \sigma e^{-\kappa t} \int_0^t e^{\kappa s} dB_s. \quad (13)$$

Therefore, we define a new time-uniform state variable, i.e. without a drift, as

$$\begin{cases} S_t = X_t + S_0 e^{-\kappa t} + b(1 - e^{-\kappa t}) \\ \text{with } X_t = \sigma e^{-\kappa t} \int_0^t e^{\kappa s} dB_s - [S_0 e^{-\kappa t} + b(1 - e^{-\kappa t})] \end{cases} \quad (14)$$

Instead of estimating the price of a vanilla option as proposed in [11], we are interested to estimate the future probability of an event using the Q-learning algorithm and a digital function. First, we define the terminal condition reflecting that with the following equation

$$Q_T^*(X_T, a_T = 0) = -\Pi_T - \lambda Var\left[\Pi_T(X_T)\right] \quad (15)$$

where Π_T is the digital function at time $t = T$ defined such that

$$\Pi_T = 1_{S_T \geq K} = \begin{cases} 1 \text{ if } S_T \geq K \\ 0 \text{ otherwise} \end{cases} \quad (16)$$

and the second term, $\lambda Var\left[\Pi_T(X_T)\right]$, is a regularization term with $\lambda \in \mathbb{R}^+ \ll 0$.

We use a backward loop to determine the value of Π_t for $t = T - 1, ..., 0$.

$$\Pi_t = \gamma \left(\Pi_{t+1} - a_t \Delta S_t \right) \quad \text{with} \quad \Delta S_t = S_{t+1} - \frac{S_t}{\gamma} = S_{t+1} - e^{r \Delta t} S_t \qquad (17)$$

Following the definition of the equations (6) and (17), we express the one-step time dependent random reward with respect to the cross-sectional information $\mathcal{F}_t$ as follows.

$$R_t(X_t, a_t, X_{t+1}) = \gamma a_t \Delta S_t(X_t, X_{t+1}) - \lambda Var\left[\Pi_t | \mathcal{F}_t\right]$$
$$\text{with } Var\left[\Pi_t | \mathcal{F}_t\right] = \gamma^2 \mathbb{E}_t \left[\hat{\Pi}_{t+1}^2 - 2a_t \Delta \hat{S}_t \hat{\Pi}_{t+1} + a_t^2 \Delta \hat{S}_t^2 \right] \qquad (18)$$

The term $\Delta \bar{S}_t$ is defined such that $\Delta \bar{S}_t = \frac{1}{N} \Delta S$, $\Delta \hat{S} = \Delta S - \Delta \bar{S}_t$ and $\hat{\Pi}_{t+1} = \Pi_{t+1} - \bar{\Pi}_{t+1}$ with $\bar{\Pi}_{t+1} = \frac{1}{N} \Pi_{t+1}$. Because of the regularizer term, the expected reward R_t is quadratic in a_t and has a finite solution. Therefore, we inject the one-step time dependent random reward equation (18) into the Bellman optimality Eq. (10) to obtain the following Q-learning update, Q^*, and the optimal action, a^*, to be solved within a backward loop $\forall t = T - 1, ..., 0$.

$$Q_t^*(X_t, a_t) = \gamma \mathbb{E}_t \left[Q_{t+1}^*(X_{t+1}, a_{t+1}^*) + a_t \Delta S_t \right] - \lambda Var\left[\Pi_t | \mathcal{F}_t\right]$$
$$a_t^*(X_t) = \mathbb{E}_t \left[\Delta \hat{S}_t \hat{\Pi}_{t+1} + \frac{1}{2\lambda\gamma} \Delta S_t \right] \left[\mathbb{E}_t \left[\left(\Delta \hat{S}_t \right)^2 \right] \right]^{-1} \qquad (19)$$

We refer to [11] for further details about the analytical solution, a^*, of the Q-learning update (19). Our approach uses the N Monte Carlo paths simultaneously to determine the optimal action a^* and the optimal action-value function Q^* to learn the policy π^*. Thus, we do not need an explicit conditioning of X_t at time t. We assume a set of basis function $\{\Phi_n(x)\}$ for which the optimal action $a_t^*(X_t)$ and the optimal action-value function, $Q_t^*(X_t, a_t^*)$, can be expanded.

$$a_t^*(X_t) = \sum_n^M \phi_{nt} \Phi_n(X_t) \quad \text{and} \quad Q_t^*(X_t, a_t^*) = \sum_n^M \omega_{nt} \Phi_n(X_t) \qquad (20)$$

The coefficients ϕ and ω are computed recursively backward in time $\forall t = T - 1, \ldots, 0$. Subsequently, we define the minimization problem to evaluate ϕ_{nt}.

$$G_t(\phi) = \sum_{k=1}^N \left[-\sum_n^M \phi_{nt} \Phi_n(X_t^k) \Delta S_t^k + \gamma \lambda \left(\Pi_{t+1}^k - \sum_n^M \phi_{nt} \Phi_n(X_t^k) \Delta \hat{S}_t^k \right)^2 \right] \qquad (21)$$

The Eq. (21) leads to the following set of linear equations $\forall n = 1, \ldots, M$.

$$\begin{cases} A_{nm}^{(t)} = \sum_{k=1}^N \Phi_n(X_t^k) \Phi_m(X_t^k) (\Delta \hat{S}_{t^k})^2 \\ B_n^{(t)} = \sum_{k=1}^N \Phi_n(X_t^k) \left[\hat{\Pi}_{t+1}^k \Delta \hat{S}_t^k + \frac{1}{2\gamma\lambda} \Delta S_t^k \right] \end{cases} \quad \text{with} \quad \sum_m^M A_{nm}^{(t)} \phi_{mt} = B_n^{(t)} \qquad (22)$$

Therefore, the coefficients of the optimal action $a_t^*(X_t)$ is determined by

$$\phi_t^* = A_t^{-1} B_t. \tag{23}$$

Hereinafter, we use Fitted Q Iteration (FQI) [19,20] to evaluate the coefficients ω. The optimal action-value function, $Q^*(X_t, a_t)$, is represented in its matrix form according to the basis function expansion of the Eq. (20).

$$Q_t^*(X_t, a_t) = \left(1, a, \frac{1}{2}a_t^2\right) \begin{pmatrix} W_{11}(t) \ W_{12}(t) \ \dots \ W_{1M}(t) \\ W_{21}(t) \ W_{22}(t) \ \dots \ W_{2M}(t) \\ W_{31}(t) \ W_{32}(t) \ \dots \ W_{3M}(t) \end{pmatrix} \begin{pmatrix} \Phi_1(X_t) \\ \vdots \\ \Phi_M(X_t) \end{pmatrix} \tag{24}$$

$$= A_t^T W_t \Phi(X_t) = A_t^T U_W(t, X_t)$$

Based on the least-square optimization problem, the coefficient W_t are determined using backpropagation $\forall t = T - 1, ..., 0$ as follows

$$\mathcal{L}_t(W_t) = \sum_{k=1}^{N} \left(R_t(X_t, a_t, X_{t+1}) + \gamma \max_{a_{t+1} \in \mathcal{A}} Q_{t+1}^*(X_{t+1}, a_{t+1}) - W_t \Psi_t(X_t, a_t) \right)^2$$

$$\text{with } W_t \Psi(X_t, a_t) + \epsilon \xrightarrow[\epsilon \to 0]{} R_t(X_t, a_t, X_{t+1}) + \gamma \max_{a_{t+1} \in \mathcal{A}} Q_{t+1}^*(X_{t+1}, a_{t+1}) \tag{25}$$

for which we derive the following set of linear equations.

$$\begin{cases} M_n^{(t)} = \sum_{k=1}^{N} \Psi_n(X_t^k, a_t^k) \left[\eta \left(R_t(X_t, a_t, X_{t+1}) + \gamma \max_{a_{t+1} \in \mathcal{A}} Q_{t+1}^*(X_{t+1}, a_{t+1}) \right) \right] \\ \text{with } \eta \sim B(N, p) \end{cases} \tag{26}$$

The term $B(N, p)$ represents the binomial distribution for n samples with probability p. It plays the role of a dropout function when evaluating the matrix M_t to compensate the well-known drawback of the Q-learning algorithm that is the overestimation of the Q-function values. We reach finally the definition of the optimal weights to determine the optimal action a^*.

$$W_t^* = S_t^{-1} M_t \tag{27}$$

The proposed model does not require any assumption on the dynamics of the time series, neither transition probabilities nor policy or reward functions. It is an off-policy model-free approach. The computation of the optimal policy, the optimal action and the optimal Q-function that leads to the future event probabilities is summed up in Algorithm 1.

Algorithm 1. Q-learning to evaluate the optimal policy of money management

---

    Data: time series of maturity T, either from generated or true data

    Result: optimal Q-function Q^*, optimal action a^*, value of digital function Π

1 **begin**

2   /*Condition at T^*/

3      $a_T^*(X_T) = 0$

4      $Q_T(X_T, a_T) = -\Pi_T = -1_{S_T \geq K}$ using Eq. (16)

5      $Q_T^*(X_T, a_T^*) = Q_T(X_T, a_T)$

6   /*Backward Loop*/

7   **for** $t \leftarrow T - 1$ **to** 0 **do**

8   /*Evaluate the coefficients ϕ^*/

9   compute A_t, B_t using Eq. (22)

10          $\phi_t^* \leftarrow A_t^{-1} B_t$

11   /*Evaluate the coefficients ω^*/

12   compute S_t, M_t using Eq. (26)

13          $W_t^* \leftarrow S_t^{-1} M_t$

14          $a_t^*(X_t) = \sum_n^M \phi_{nt}^* \Phi_n(X_t)$

15          $Q^*(X_t, a_t) = A_t^T W_t^* \Phi_((X_t)$

16   /*Compute the digital function value to estimate the event probability at $t = 0$*/

17   print($\Pi_0 = mean(Q_0^*)$)

18 **return**

---

4 Experiments

We empirically evaluate the performance of MQLV. We initially highlight the similarities between historical payment transactions and Vasicek generated transactions. We then underline the MQLV's capabilities to learn the optimal policy of money management based on the estimation of future event probabilities in comparison to the closed formula of [12,13], hereinafter denoted by BSM's closed formula. We rely on synthetic data sets because of the privacy and the confidentiality issues of the retail banking data sets.

Data Availability and Data Description. One of our contributions is to bring a RL framework designed for retail banking. However, none of the data sets can be released publicly because of the highly sensitive information they contain. We therefore show the similarities between a small sample of anonymized transactions and Vasicek generated transactions [16]. We then use the Vasicek mean reverting stochastic diffusion process to generate larger synthetic data sets similar to the original retail banking data sets. The mean reverting dynamic is particularly interesting since it reflects a wide range of retail banking transactions including the credit card transactions, the savings history or the clients' spendings. Three different data sets were generated to avoid any bias that could have been introduced by using only one data set. We choose to differentiate the number of Monte Carlo paths between the data sets to assess the influence of the sampling size on the results. The first, second and third data sets contain respectively 20,000, 30,000 and 40,000 paths. We release publicly the data sets[1] to ensure the reproducibility of the experiments.

Experimental Setup and Code Availability. In our experiments, we generate synthetic data sets using the Vasicek model with a parameter $S_0 = 1.0$ corresponding to the value of the time series at $t = 0$, a maturity of six months $T = 0.5$, a speed reversion $a = 0.01$, a long term mean $b = 1$ and a volatility $\sigma = 0.15$. Because the choice of the parameters of the Vasicek model do not have any influence on the results of the Q-learning approach, the numbers were fixed such that any limitations of the methodology would be quickly observed. The number of time steps is fixed equal to 5. We additionally use different strike values for the experiments explicitly mentioned in the Results and Discussions subsection. The simulations were performed on a computer with 16GB of RAM, Intel i7 CPU and a Tesla K80 GPU accelerator. To ensure the reproducibility of the experiments, the code is available at the following address[1].

Results and Discussions about MQLV. As aforementioned, we cannot release publicly an anonymized transactions data set because of privacy, confidentiality and regulatory issues. We consequently highlight the similarities between the dynamic of a small sample of anonymized transactions and Vasicek generated transactions for one client [21] in Fig. 1. The financial transactions in retail banking are periodic and often fluctuates around a long term mean, reflecting the frequency and the amounts of the spendings habits of the clients. The akin dynamic of the original and the generated transactions is highlighted by the small RMSE of 0.03. We also performed a least square calibration of the Vasicek parameters to assess the model's plausibility. We can observe in Table 1 that the Vasicek parameters have the same magnitude and, therefore, it supports the hypothesis that the Vasicek model could be used to generate synthetic transactions.

We present the core of our contribution in the following experiment. We aim at learning the optimal policy of money management. It is particularly interesting for bank loan applications where the differences between a client's spendings policy and the optimal policy can be compared. We show that MQLV is capable of evaluating accurately the probability of a default event using a digital function which highlights the learning of the optimal policy of money management. Effectively, if the MQLV's learned policy is different than the optimal policy, then the probabilities of default events are not accurate. In Fig. 2, the estimation of future event probabilities for different strike values is represented. We rely on the BSM's closed formula for the vanilla option pricing [12,13] to

---

[1] The code and the data sets are available at https://github.com/dagrate/MQLV.

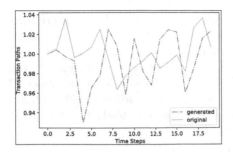

Fig. 1. Samples of original and Vasicek generated transactions for one client. The two samples oscillate around a long term mean of 1 and have a similar pattern, highlighted by the small RMSE of 0.03 in Table 1.

Table 1. RMSE error between the samples of original transactions and generated Vasicek transactions of Fig. 1. We also calibrated the Vasicek parameters according to the original transactions to validate the model's plausibility.

Description	Value
RMSE	0.0335
Vasicek speed reversion a	0.5444
Vasicek long term mean b	0.9001
Vasicek volatility σ	0.2185

approximate the digital function values [15]. We used, therefore, the BSM's values as reference values to cross-validate the MQLV's values. MQLV achieves a close representation of the event probabilities for the different strike values in Fig. 2. The curves of both the MQLV and the BSM's approaches are similar with a RMSE of 1.5016. This result highlights that the learned Q-learning policy of MQLV is sufficiently close to the optimal policy to compute event probabilities almost identical to the probabilities of the BSM's formula approximation.

We gathered quantitative results in Table 2 for a deeper analysis of the MQLV's results. The event probability values are listed for the three data sets. We chose a set of parameters for the Vasicek model such that our configuration is free of any time-dependency. We therefore expect a probability value of 50% at a threshold of 1 because the standard deviation of the generated data sets is only induced by the normal distribution standard deviation, used to simulate the Brownian motion. Surprisingly, the MQLV values at a strike of 1 are closer to 50% than the BSM's values for all the data sets. We can conclude, subsequently, that, for our configuration, MQLV is capable to learn the optimal policy of money management which is reflected by the accurate evaluation of the event probabilities.

We chose to generate three new data sets with new Vasicek parameters a and σ to underline the potential of MQLV and the universality of the results. In Table 3, we computed the event probabilities for different strikes for the newly generated data sets. The parameter b remains unchanged since we want to keep a configuration free of any time-dependency. We notice that MQLV is capable to estimate a probability of 50% for a strike of 1 which can only be obtained if MQLV is able to learn the optimal policy. We also observe that the BSM's approximation does lead to a lower accuracy. We showed in this experiment that our model-free and off-policy RL approach, MQLV, is able to learn the optimal policy reflected by the accurate probability values independently of the data sets considered and of the Vasicek parameters.

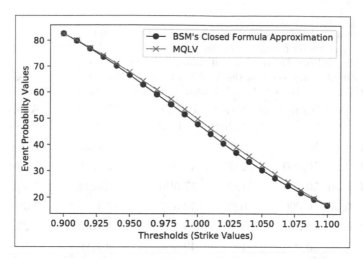

Fig. 2. Event probability values calculated by MQLV and BSM's closed formula approximation for 40,000 Monte Carlo paths with Vasicek parameters $a = 0.01, b = 1$ and $\sigma = 0.15$. The BSM's closed formula approximation values are used as reference values. The event probabilities of MQLV are close to the BSM's values with a total RMSE of 1.502. It illustrates that MQLV is able to learn the optimal policy leading to accurate event probabilities.

Table 2. Valuation differences of the digital values for event probabilities according to different strikes between the BSM's closed formula approximation and MQLV. Given our time-uniform configuration, the event probability values should be close to 50% for a strike value of 1. The MQLV values are close to the theoretical target of 50% at a strike of 1 highlighting the MQLV's capabilities to learn the optimal policy. The BSM's closed formula approximation slightly underestimates the probability values.

Data set	Number of paths	Strike values	BSM's approx. values (%)	MQLV values (%)	Absolute difference
1	20,000	0.92	76.810	**77.098**	0.288
1	20,000	0.98	55.447	**57.920**	2.473
1	20,000	1.00	47.867	**50.235**	2.368
1	20,000	1.02	40.509	**42.865**	2.356
2	30,000	0.92	76.810	**76.953**	0.143
2	30,000	0.98	55.447	**57.760**	2.313
2	30,000	1.00	47.867	**50.043**	2.176
2	30,000	1.02	40.509	**42.744**	2.235
3	40,000	0.92	76.810	**77.047**	0.237
3	40,000	0.98	55.447	**57.491**	2.044
3	40,000	1.00	47.867	**49.924**	2.057
3	40,000	1.02	40.509	**42.713**	2.204

Table 3. Event probabilities for data sets generated with different Vasicek parameters a and σ. The parameter b remains unchanged to keep a configuration free of any time-dependency to facilitate the results explainability. We can deduce that MQLV is able to learn the optimal policy because the MQLV's probabilities are close to the theoretical target of 50% at a strike of 1. MQLV is also more accurate than BSM's formula.

Parameters $a; b; \sigma$	Number of Paths	Strike Values	BSM's App. Values (%)	MQLV Values (%)	Absolute Difference
0.01; 1; 0.10	50,000	0.98	59.856	**61.223**	1.366
0.01; 1; 0.10	50,000	1.00	48.562	**50.001**	1.439
0.01; 1; 0.10	50,000	1.02	37.596	**39.044**	1.447
0.01; 1; 0.30	50,000	0.98	49.558	**53.647**	4.089
0.01; 1; 0.30	50,000	1.00	45.767	**49.997**	4.230
0.01; 1; 0.30	50,000	1.02	42.088	**46.194**	4.106
0.10; 1; 0.15	50,000	0.98	55.447	**57.540**	2.093
0.10; 1; 0.15	50,000	1.00	47.867	**50.015**	2.148
0.10; 1; 0.15	50,000	1.02	40.509	**42.638**	2.129
0.30; 1; 0.15	50,000	0.98	55.447	**57.586**	2.139
0.30; 1; 0.15	50,000	1.00	47.867	**50.022**	2.155
0.30; 1; 0.15	50,000	1.02	40.509	**42.542**	2.033

Limitations of the BSM's Closed Formula Used for Cross Validation. In our experiments, we observed, surprisingly, that the BSM's closed formula approximation underestimates the event probability values. The volatility is the only parameter playing a significant role in the generation of the time series and, therefore, the event probability should be equal to the mean of the distribution used to generate the random numbers. The Brownian motion is simulated with a standard normal distribution with a 0.5 mean. The BSM's closed formula did not, however, lead to a probability of 0.5 but to slightly smaller values because of the limit of their theoretical framework [12, 13]. Hence, we observed that MQLV was more accurate than the BSM's closed formula in our configuration.

5   Related Work

The foundations of modern reinforcement learning described in [2, 4] established the theoretical framework to learn good policies for sequential decision problems by proposing a formulation of cumulative future reward signal. The Q-learning algorithm introduced in [3] is one of the cornerstone of all recent reinforcement learning publications. However, the convergence of the Q-Learning algorithm was solved several years later. It was shown that the Q-Learning algorithm with non-linear function approximators [22] with off-policy learning [23] could provoke a divergence of the Q-network. Therefore, the reinforcement learning community focused on linear function approximators [22] to ensure convergence.

The emergence of neural networks and deep learning [24] contributed to address the use of reinforcement learning with neural networks. At an early stage, deep auto-encoders were used to extract feature spaces to solve reinforcement learning tasks [25]. Then, thanks to the release of the Atari 2600 emulator [26], a public data set was available answering the needs of the RL community for larger simulation. The Atari emulator allowed a proper performance benchmark of the different reinforcement learning algorithms and offered the possibility to test various architectures. The Atari games were used to introduce the concept of deep reinforcement learning [1,7]. The authors used a convolutional neural network trained with a variant of Q-learning to successfully learn control policies directly from high dimensional sensory inputs. They reached human-level performance on many of the Atari games. Shortly after, the deep reinforcement learning was challenged by double Q-Learning within a deep reinforcement learning framework [9]. The double Q-Learning algorithm was initially introduced in [19] in a tabular setting. The double deep Q-Learning gave more accurate estimates and lead to much higher scores than the one observed in [1,7]. Consequently, an ongoing work is to further improve the results of the double deep Q-learning algorithms through different variants. In [27], the authors used a quantile regression to approximate the full quantile function for the state-action return distribution, leading to a large class of risk-sensitive policies. It allowed them to further improve the scores on the Atari 2600 games simulator. Similarly, a new algorithm, called C51, which applies the Bellman's equation to the learning of the approximate value distribution was designed in [28]. They showed state-of-the-art results on the Atari 2600 emulator.

Other publications meanwhile focused on model-free policies and actor-critic framework. Stochastic policies were trained in [29] with a replay buffer to avoid divergence. It was showed in [30] that deterministic policy gradients (DPG) exist, even in a model-free environment. Subsequently, the DPG approach was extended in [31] using a deviator network. Continuous control policies were learned using backpropagation introducing the Stochastic Value Gradient SVG(0) and SVG(1) in [32]. Recently, Deep Deterministic Policy Gradient (DDPG) was presented in [10] to learn competitive policies using an actor-critic model-free algorithm based on the DPG that operates over continuous action spaces.

6   Conclusion

We introduced Modified Q-Learning for Vasicek or MQLV, a new model-free and off-policy reinforcement learning approach capable of evaluating an optimal policy of money management based on the aggregated transactions of the clients. MQLV is part of a banking strategy that looks to minimize the customer churn by including more transparency and more personalization in the decision process related to bank loan applications or credit card limits. It relies on a digital function to estimate the future probability of an event such as a payment default. We discuss its relation with the Bellman optimality equation and the Q-learning update. We conducted experiments on synthetic data sets because of the privacy and confidentiality issues related to the retail banking data sets. The generated data sets followed a mean reverting stochastic diffusion process, the Vasicek model, simulating retail banking data sets such as transaction payments. Our experiments showed the performance of MQLV with respect to the BSM's closed formula for vanilla options. We also highlighted that MQLV is able to determine an optimal policy, an optimal Q-function, optimal actions and optimal states reflected by accurate probabilities. Surprisingly, we observed that MQLV led to more accurate event probabilities than the popular BSM's formula.

Future work will address the creation of a fully anonymized data set illustrating the retail banking daily transactions with a privacy, confidentiality and regulatory compliance. We will also evaluate the MQLV's performance for data sets that violate the Vasicek assumptions. We, furthermore, observed that the Q-learning update could minor the real probability values for simulation involving a small temporal discretization such as $\Delta t = 200$. Preliminary results showed it is provoked by the basis function approximator error. We will address this point in future research. Finally, we will extend the Q-learning update to other scheme for improved accuracy and incorporate a deep learning framework.

References

1. Mnih, V., et al.: Playing atari with deep reinforcement learning. arXiv preprint arXiv:1312.5602 (2013)
2. Sutton, R.S.: Temporal credit assignment in reinforcement learning (1984)
3. Watkins, C.J.C.H.: Learning from delayed rewards. Ph.D. thesis, King's College, Cambridge (1989)
4. Williams, R.: A class of gradient-estimation algorithms for reinforcement learning in neural networks. In: Proceedings of the International Conference on Neural Networks, pp. II-601 (1987)
5. Krizhevsky, A., Sutskever, I., Hinton, G.E.: Imagenet classification with deep convolutional neural networks. In: Advances in Neural Information Processing Systems, pp. 1097–1105 (2012)
6. Sermanet, P., Kavukcuoglu, K., Chintala, S., LeCun, Y.: Pedestrian detection with unsupervised multi-stage feature learning. In: Proceedings of the IEEE Conference on Computer Vision and Pattern Recognition, pp. 3626–3633 (2013)
7. Mnih, V., et al.: Human-level control through deep reinforcement learning. Nature **518**(7540), 529 (2015)
8. Watkins, C.J., Dayan, P.: Q-learning. Mach. Learn. **8**(3–4), 279–292 (1992)
9. Van Hasselt, H., Guez, A., Silver, D.: Deep reinforcement learning with double q-learning. In: AAAI, Phoenix, AZ, vol. 2, p. 5 (2016)
10. Lillicrap, T.P., et al.: Continuous control with deep reinforcement learning. arXiv preprint arXiv:1509.02971 (2015)
11. Halperin, I.: Qlbs: Q-learner in the black-scholes (-merton) worlds. arXiv preprint arXiv:1712.04609 (2017)
12. Black, F., Scholes, M.: The pricing of options and corporate liabilities. J. Polit. Econ. **81**(3), 637–654 (1973)

13. Merton, R.C.: Theory of rational option pricing. Bell J. Econ. Manag. Sci. **4**, 141–183 (1973)
14. Wilmott, P.: Paul Wilmott on Quantitative Finance. Wiley, Hoboken (2013)
15. Hull, J.C.: Options Futures and Other Derivatives. Pearson Education India, Bengaluru (2003)
16. Vasicek, O.: An equilibrium characterization of the term structure. J. Financ. Econ. **5**(2), 177–188 (1977)
17. Sutton, R.S., Barto, A.G.: Reinforcement Learning: An Introduction. MIT Press, Cambridge (2018)
18. Robbins, H., Monro, S.: A stochastic approximation method. In: Herbert Robbins Selected Papers, pp. 102–109. Springer, Heidelberg (1985)
19. Hasselt, H.V.: Double q-learning. In: Advances in Neural Information Processing Systems, pp. 2613–2621 (2010)
20. Murphy, S.A.: A generalization error for Q-learning. J. Mach. Learn. Res. **6**(Jul), 1073–1097 (2005)
21. Santander: Santander product recommendation (2016). https://www.kaggle.com/c/santander-product-recommendation/data
22. Tsitsiklis, J.N., Van Roy, B.: Analysis of temporal-diffference learning with function approximation. In: Advances in Neural Information Processing Systems, pp. 1075–1081 (1997)
23. Baird, L.: Residual algorithms: reinforcement learning with function approximation. In: Machine Learning Proceedings 1995, pp. 30–37. Elsevier (1995)
24. Goodfellow, I., Bengio, Y., Courville, A., Bengio, Y.: Deep Learning, vol. 1. MIT Press, Cambridge (2016)
25. Lange, S., Riedmiller, M.: Deep auto-encoder neural networks in reinforcement learning. In: The 2010 International Joint Conference on Neural Networks (IJCNN), pp. 1–8. IEEE (2010)
26. Bellemare, M.G., Naddaf, Y., Veness, J., Bowling, M.: The arcade learning environment: an evaluation platform for general agents. J. Artif. Intell. Res. **47**, 253–279 (2013)
27. Dabney, W., Ostrovski, G., Silver, D., Munos, R.: Implicit quantile networks for distributional reinforcement learning. arXiv preprint arXiv:1806.06923 (2018)
28. Bellemare, M.G., Dabney, W., Munos, R.: A distributional perspective on reinforcement learning. arXiv preprint arXiv:1707.06887 (2017)
29. Wawrzyński, P., Tanwani, A.K.: Autonomous reinforcement learning with experience replay. Neural Netw. **41**, 156–167 (2013)
30. Silver, D., Lever, G., Heess, N., Degris, T., Wierstra, D., Riedmiller, M.: Deterministic policy gradient algorithms. In: ICML (2014)
31. Balduzzi, D., Ghifary, M.: Compatible value gradients for reinforcement learning of continuous deep policies. arXiv preprint arXiv:1509.03005 (2015)
32. Heess, N., Wayne, G., Silver, D., Lillicrap, T., Erez, T., Tassa, Y.: Learning continuous control policies by stochastic value gradients. In: Advances in Neural Information Processing Systems, pp. 2944–2952 (2015)

Curriculum Learning in Deep Neural Networks for Financial Forecasting

Allison Koenecke[1,2](✉) [iD] and Amita Gajewar[2]

[1] Stanford University, Stanford, CA 94305, USA
koenecke@stanford.edu
[2] Microsoft Corp., Sunnyvale, CA 94089, USA
amitag@microsoft.com

Abstract. For any financial organization, computing accurate quarterly forecasts for various products is one of the most critical operations. As the granularity at which forecasts are needed increases, traditional statistical time series models may not scale well. We apply deep neural networks in the forecasting domain by experimenting with techniques from Natural Language Processing (Encoder-Decoder LSTMs) and Computer Vision (Dilated CNNs), as well as incorporating transfer learning. A novel contribution of this paper is the application of curriculum learning to neural network models built for time series forecasting. We illustrate the performance of our models using Microsoft's revenue data corresponding to Enterprise, and Small, Medium & Corporate products, spanning approximately 60 regions across the globe for 8 different business segments, and totaling in the order of tens of billions of USD. We compare our models' performance to the ensemble model (of traditional statistics and machine learning) currently being used by Microsoft Finance. Using this in-production model as a baseline, our experiments yield an approximately 30% improvement overall in accuracy on test data. We find that our curriculum learning LSTM-based model performs best, which shows that one can implement our proposed methods without overfitting on medium-sized data.

Keywords: Financial forecasting · LSTM · Dilated CNN · Curriculum learning · Time series

1 Introduction

A key aspect of effective business planning is the ability to accurately forecast finances. This paper is the result of a partnership with Microsoft's Finance team to provide them guidance on projected revenue for both their Enterprise, and Small, Medium & Corporate (SMC) Groups.

Our goal is to forecast the revenue for Microsoft products, wherein the worldwide revenue is partitioned into 8 different segments; examples of segments

Supported by Microsoft Corp., where all research was conducted.

V. Bitetta et al. (Eds.): MIDAS 2019, LNAI 11985, pp. 16–31, 2020.
https://doi.org/10.1007/978-3-030-37720-5_2

include Commercial Enterprise or SMC Education. Each segment is further partitioned into approximately 60 regions, and each region's revenue is then partitioned further into 20 different products. We henceforth refer to each combination of segment, region, and product as a "datarow". Overall, there are approximately 6,000 datarows (since not all products are sold in all regions), with each datarow corresponding to a time series used for our forecasting problem.

The forecasting models currently used by the Finance team are built using traditional time series and machine learning models [6]. Here, we extend the capability to forecast product revenue at a more granular level, with improved accuracy and efficiency. As data become more granular, further insights can be made by the sales team. However, this comes with obvious challenges in training any machine learning model: the historical length of revenue information available may vary across sub-levels, and data itself can become noisy for different sub-levels. In these cases, fitting a statistical time series model to individual time series may not necessarily yield accurate forecasts, nor would this be a scalable solution. Following recent advances in applying deep neural networks (DNNs) in the time series domain [9], this paper explores applying Long Short-Term Memory (LSTM) and Dilated Convolutional Neural Network (DCNN) models to hierarchical financial time series.

In the following sections, we describe the advancements made from prior work, our data structure, and the two overarching DNN models used (LSTM and DCNN). Specifically, we describe the incremental accuracy gains from pre-processing techniques and additional features included in each DNN model, highlighting the performance of Curriculum Learning as described below. Lastly, we interpret results and discuss implications and future steps. By comparing against Microsoft's production baseline accuracy, we find that our curriculum learning method can be successfully applied to various neural networks on time series data to achieve higher accuracy and positive results in bias and variance.

2   Related Work

Sequence-to-sequence modeling for time series has been fairly popular for the past several years, not just in industry, but also broadly from classrooms [16] to Kaggle [17]. These methods range from vanilla models to advanced industry competitors.

There are three major differentiating features between our research and previous related work on time series forecasting. First, curriculum learning (as defined below) has not yet been applied to time series trends. Second, we highlight the transfer learning occurring within-task, from datarows having enough historical data to train effectively, to datarows lacking the amount of historical data needed to serve as model inputs. Third, while deep learning models implemented in industry are mostly applied to "big data", this paper shows that both Recurrent Neural Networks (RNNs) and Convolutional Neural Networks (CNNs) can be used effectively on medium-sized data without overfitting.

We first address the previous work on curriculum learning, which is essentially changing the order of inputs to a model to improve results. The intuition from Natural Language Processing (NLP) regarding this method is that shorter sentences are easier to learn than longer sentences; so, without initialization, one can bootstrap via iterated learning in order of increasing sentence length. The relevant literature, including specifically the described Baby Steps algorithm [2,13], has been applied to LSTMs for parsing a Wall Street Journal corpus [13], n-gram language modeling [7], and for performing digit sums using LSTMs [4]. However, there has been no application of this work to real numerical time series data.

We next comment on how we have utilized the concept of transfer learning in our work. While there has been work done on transfer learning across tasks for CNNs [8] and RNNs [10], as well as research on meta-learning across time series [15], there has not yet been an extensively applied example showing the ability to ameliorate the missing data problem by forecasting one datarow using historical trends from (in our case) a different region, segment, or product. Prior work on similar transfer learning focuses on robustness of out-of-sample test results and testing predictions at different timesteps [12], which does not account for missing data and is relatively infeasible to reproduce given the much smaller size of the Microsoft data. We discuss implications at length in Sect. 6.

Lastly, we turn to previous instances of using neural networks to forecast time series data. While it is fairly straightforward to use neural networks on large datasets, it is more difficult to apply these techniques to small and medium-sized data due to the risk of overfitting. Many companies have adopted the use of LSTMs for time series modeling, but arguably the most advanced public methodology comes from Uber, which won the 2018 M4 Forecasting Competition using a hybrid Exponential Smoothing and RNN model [11]. Their work shares many basic elements with our work: a rolling window train and validation method; data preprocessing methods that involve deseasonalization; and the use of LSTMs. However, Uber's application is quite different: first, their data are orders of magnitude larger than ours, and second, their data do not contain similarly rigid hierarchical elements (rather, their vast number of covariates necessitates an autoencoder for feature extraction). Another proven neural network method for financial forecasting is the Dilated CNN [3], wherein the underlying architecture comes from DeepMind's WaveNet project [18]. This prior work is again on data much larger than ours, and also does not specify or discuss many data pre-processing steps (after audio pre-processing, WaveNet simply quantizes to a fixed range). However, we have found that certain pre-processing techniques, such as log-transformation of de-meaned values and de-seasonalization, can be crucial to improving accuracy.

3 Data

3.1 Data Structure

As noted in Sect. 1, world-wide revenues for Enterprise and SMC groups are partitioned into 8 business segments; each segment is partitioned into approximately 60 regions, and each region's revenue is partitioned further into 20 different products. Given historical quarterly revenue data, our goal is to forecast quarterly revenue for these products per combination of product, segment, and region; we then generate the aggregated segment-level forecasts as well as worldwide aggregates. Note that we focus on segment-level (rather than subregion or product-level) forecasts for comparison's sake, since this level has historically been used by the business. All revenue numbers are adjusted to be in USD currency using a constant exchange rate. Sample datarow structure is presented in Fig. 1.

Group	SubRegionName	CustomSubsegment	CustomSRSD	2009-01-01 00:00:00	2009-04-01 00:00:00	2009-07-01 00:00:00	2009-10-01 00:00:00	2010-01-01 00:00:00
0 Argentina . Commercial Enterprise . Developer ...	Argentina	Commercial Enterprise	Developer Tools					
1 Argentina . Commercial Enterprise . Dynamics O...	Argentina	Commercial Enterprise	Dynamics OnPrem					

Fig. 1. Sample datarow structure excluding financial values

We use the quarterly revenue available (post-data-processing) for each datarow over fiscal quarters from January 2009 through July 2018 (totaling 39 timesteps). Broadly speaking, we train on the first 35 timesteps of all datarows, and test on the final 4 timesteps; details are presented in the following section.

For all DNN models, we train on a subset of the data which has good enough history to fit a reasonable model. Post-training, we apply this model to forecast revenue both for datarows on which it was trained, and also on out-of-sample datarows that were not seen by the model at the time of training due to insufficient historical information. Specifically, we perform basic data cleaning, and then use a subset of datarows (approximately 84% of all datarows) containing sufficient history for model training. We later apply transfer learning to the remaining out-of-sample datarows (approximately 16% of all datarows). Our results are evaluated by calculating Mean Absolute Percentage Error (MAPE) at the segment and world-wide level.

3.2 Microsoft Baseline

Circa 2015, most of the revenue forecasting in Microsoft's Finance division was driven by human judgement. In order to explore more efficient, accurate and unbiased revenue forecasting, machine learning methodology was explored along with statistical time series models [1]. The methodology described in [1] was used to compute forecasts in 13 worldwide regions. In [6], this approach was further extended to use product level data available within each region, and to generate forecasts for each product within region (allowing for aggregation to region-level and world-wide forecasts). This is the approach that is currently adopted by Microsoft's Finance team; models based on this approach are running in a production environment to generate quarterly revenue forecasts to be used by Finance team members. The results obtained from this method are referred to as the Microsoft baseline, and this paper explores whether the proposed DNN-based models can outperform the current baseline model in production. For the ease of understanding the baseline model referred to in this paper, we describe here the methodology in [6] at a high level.

A product's historical revenue information varies depending on the age and popularity of the product; hence, it is not possible to naively apply single time series or machine learning model for all products, and still obtain accurate results. For very new products (having fewer than 6 quarters of revenue data), a simple heuristic is used. Otherwise, products are divided into three categories depending on the amount of historical revenue information available:

1. Products with more than 20 quarters of revenue data. Microsoft uses a combined approach of various time series and machine learning models with cross validation for hyper-parameter tuning, where the final forecast generated corresponds to one of the time series (e.g., ARIMA, ETS and STL) or machine learning models (e.g., Random Forest, ElasticNet, etc.) that had the lowest historical error as computed on the validation dataset.
2. Products with between 14 and 19 quarters of revenue data. Only statistical time series models are fit. Derived features are also constructed from these time series models, e.g., the average of the ETS-forecast and ARIMA-forecast can be used as an additional forecasted data point.
3. Products with between 6 and 13 quarters of revenue data. Only ARIMA and ETS statistical time series models are fit, as STL cannot be trained on very short time series. Since there is not enough history available to set aside a validation dataset, the final forecast is the simple average of the ARIMA-forecast and ETS-forecast.

In aggregate, the above methods described form the Microsoft baseline that will be used as a benchmark for our results described below.

4   Methods

Our work on time series is mostly inspired by non-financial applications. Specifically, Encoder-Decoder LSTMs (Sect. 4.1) are used in NLP, and Dilated CNNs (Sect. 4.2) are applied in Computer Vision and Speech Recognition.

4.1   RNN Model: Encoder-Decoder LSTM

We present four variants, each cumulatively building upon the previous variant, of our RNN model to show increasing reduction in error. In all variants, we use a walk-forward split [1] wherein validation sets are four steps forward into time from training sets, ensuring no data leakage. We do this iteratively for windows of size 15 timesteps within the data, continuously walking forward in time until the end of the training data (i.e., until July 2017); this is referred to as the rolling window process. The window size of 15 timesteps was chosen empirically. As we move from one window to the next, we use weights obtained from the model trained on data corresponding to the previous window for initialization. An example loss function when using the rolling window process is shown in Fig. 2; notice that gradual loss is attained as we step through consecutive windows because the model uses prior weights to warm-start rather than fitting from scratch.

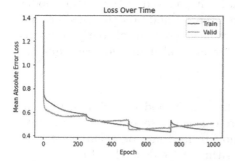

Fig. 2. Example mean absolute error loss for rolling window method on LSTM

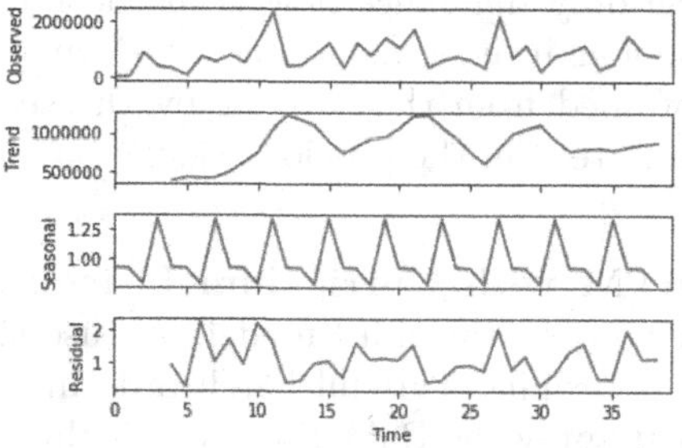

Fig. 3. Seasonal decomposition example on one financial datarow

Basic LSTM. The first model we discuss is our basic RNN model. All training, validation, and test data are historical financial values that have been smoothed using a logarithmic transformation and de-meaned on training data only. These pre-processing methods are used throughout due to better experimental results relative to other smoothing transformations. A single-layer sequence-to-sequence model is fed into a dense layer, using the Adam optimizer on mean absolute error. The sequence-to-sequence [14] architecture involves a LSTM encoder (to process revenue and return interal state), and an LSTM decoder (to use the previous time step's actual data and internal LSTM encoder states to generate the next output). Teacher forcing is used only during training; for inference, we feed in the predicted values for the next timestep as input to the decoder instead of the actual value as would be the case in the teacher forcing method. Next, we apply the inverse smoothing transformation on the decoder's output for last four timesteps (i.e., revenue for the last four quarters) to calculate test error.

LSTM with Categorical Indicators. The second model we examine is simply the basic model with additional indicator covariates (i.e., one-hot categorical variables are incorporated in the model). Specifically, for our three categorical variables (segment, region, and product), we include one-hot encodings so that the hierarchical product information is reflected in the model.

LSTM with Seasonality. The third model incorporates seasonal effects in the second model. Specifically, we use multiplicative Seasonal Trend decomposition using Loess (STL) [5] to calculate trend, seasonal, and residual components. A sample datarow decomposition is shown in Fig. 3. We extract the seasonal component from the relevant datarows, and we use only the product of trend and residual effects (in each quarter, and for each datarow) as inputs to be smoothed and fed to the neural network model. De-seasonalizing the input data along with other aforementioned transformations (logarithmic and de-meaning) helps to make the data more stationary.

We maintain use of the indicator covariates introduced in the second model. The only difference now is in the inference step: in addition to decoding and using an inverse smoothing transformation, we must also multiply our predictions obtained from the decoder by the seasonal values calculated for each quarter (timestep) in the previous year.

LSTM with Curriculum Learning. The fourth model applies curriculum learning to the third model. We use the pre-calculated seasonal decomposition to determine a useful batch ordering method to feed into our neural net, and then apply the Baby Steps curriculum algorithm [4,13] defined in Fig. 4.

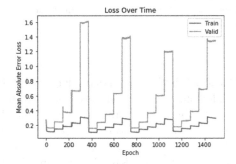

```
 1: procedure BS-CURRICULUM(M,D,C)
 2:     D' = sort(D,C)
 3:     {D¹,D²,...,Dᵏ} = D' where C(d_a) < C(d_b) d_a ∈
        Dⁱ, d_b ∈ Dʲ, ∀i < j
 4:     D^{train} = ∅
 5:     for s = 1...k do
 6:         D^{train} = D^{train} ∪ Dˢ
 7:         while not converged for p epochs do
 8:             train(M, D^{train})
 9:         end while
10:     end for
11: end procedure
```

Fig. 4. Baby steps curriculum learning algorithm [4,13]

Fig. 5. Example mean absolute error loss for curriculum learning with rolling window method on LSTM (ordered from easiest to hardest estimated prediction)

Let us define $D' = sort(D, C)$ for training data D and curriculum sort metric C [4], where our sort metric is specified as the residual trend weighted by segment revenue for each datarow. That is, we will sort our training data on this new variable we have created, which exists for each datarow. Then, we order our batches such that $\{D^1, D^2, ..., D^k\} = D'$ where $C(d_a) < C(d_b)$ for $d_a \in D^i, d_b \in D^j, \forall i < j$. In words, we train in increasing order of the residual error calculated from the STL decomposition mentioned previously. Once the k batches are defined, we shuffle the datarows within the batch during training. Within each iteration of the rolling window process, we continue the warm-start process by iteratively adding one batch at a time to the training data, running each rolling window iteration p times, where p is the number of epochs chosen such that convergence can be reached. In summary, for each of the $s = 1, ..., k$ batches, we run $D^{train} = D^{train} \cup D^s$ until the end of p epochs of each rolling window iteration. A sample loss function including curriculum learning is shown in Fig. 5, where we have experimentally chosen $p = 75$.

We note that there are several ways to form the batching described above. In our results, we present batches formed directly from the datarow sort metric calculated as described above, i.e., the datarow-level residual error (using 5 batches, as determined experimentally). However, we have also found good results when batching by segment (with each batch corresponding to one Microsoft segment), where batches are sorted by revenue-weighted segment-level residual error. In all cases, we shuffle datarows within each batch when training. The idea of curriculum learning, as highlighted in Sect. 1, is to train on easier examples to learn harder ones. As such, we find that running curriculum learning with batches sorted in order of best-fit to least-fit segments yields similar results to those that we find from the datarow-level (uniform-weighting) method we use in this paper. However, we also experimented with curriculum learning using batches sorted in reverse order: least-fit to best-fit segments. This resulted in far better accuracies for certain (smaller-revenue) segments, but worse accuracies for all other segments. Hence, it remains a reasonable option to sort in various ways, and then ensemble results, to tease out best results for different segments.

4.2   CNN Model: Dilated CNN

We present three versions of our CNN model to show increased reduction in error across iterations. We note that we do not explore separating seasonal effects from our DCNN model as a pre-processing step. While found to be useful in the LSTM model, results are not significantly better for the DCNN when performing seasonal decomposition prior to training the model. This is likely because the exponential nature of the DCNN layers allows us to capture the seasonality over a long time series, especially since we are using each relevant datarow's full 35-quarter financial history as input to the model (rather than the rolling window method applied for LSTMs).

Basic Dilated CNN. In our first Dilated CNN model, we use 1D convolutions in each of 10 dilated convolutional layers (with 6 filters of width 2 per layer). This connects to an exponential number (2^{10}) of input values for the output. Two fully connected layers are used to obtain a final output: a dense layer of size 128 with ReLU activation, and a dense layer of size 1. We apply an Adam optimizer on the Mean Absolute Error. Teacher forcing is done during training only, and predicts the four test quarters of data iteratively, appending each prediction to history for the next timestep's prediction. Similar to the LSTM model, all historical financial values passed into the DCNN model have been smoothed using a logarithmic transformation and de-meaned on training data only.

Dilated CNN with Categorical Indicators. The second DCNN model we examine is simply the above basic model with additional indicator covariates. Specifically, for our three categorical variables (segment, region, and product), we include one-hot encodings so that the hierarchical product information is reflected in the model.

Dilated CNN with Curriculum Learning. We apply the same mechanism for curriculum learning as explained for the LSTM model, using the residual from seasonal decompositions as a proxy for the difficulty of forecasting each datarow. We batch by the datarow-level residual error (using 8 batches, as determined experimentally). The curriculum learning is performed based on the second DCNN model, i.e., including categorical variables, but not using seasonal decomposition for anything aside from the sort order for curriculum learning.

4.3   Evaluation

For evaluation purposes, we use the four quarters of data from October 2017 to July 2018 as our test dataset. For certain products, there are only null values available in recent quarters (e.g., if the product is being discontinued) and hence we do not include these products in the test dataset. We use the Mean Absolute Percentage Error (MAPE) as our error evaluation metric. To take into account the inherent randomness involved from weight initialization when training the DNNs, and considering that our data is medium-sized, we run each experiment 30 times to obtain a more robust estimate of the errors. For each datarow, we take the average of the forecasts across runs and across quarters as the final forecast and compare this predicted revenue to the actual observed revenue. The segment-level forecast is the sum of all (subregion-level and product-level) forecasts falling into that segment. The world-wide forecast is the sum of forecasts for all datarows.

5   Results

We find that both LSTM and DCNN models with curriculum learning outperform the respective models without curricum learning. In particular, the Encoder-Decoder LSTM with curriculum learning (including categorical indicators and seasonality effects) yields the lowest error rates, showing a worldwide improvement of 27%, and a revenue-weighted segment-based improvement of 30%, over Microsoft's production baseline. We further find that curriculum learning models can yield either lower bias or variance for various segments.

Due to privacy concerns, actual test errors are not displayed. We instead report relative percentage improvement over the Microsoft baseline in production.

5.1   World-Wide Error Rates

World-wide MAPEs for all models are compared in Table 1. Both LSTM and DCNN models with curriculum learning outperform all variants without curriculum learning by over 10% points. It is worth noting that even the baseline LSTM model (without curriculum learning) improves upon the Microsoft baseline in production. We lastly comment on the decrease in world-wide accuracy upon adding seasonality to the LSTM model. While the world-wide error (MAPE) is higher for this model variant, we see in Table 2 that the revenue-weighted segment-level average yields an improvement of 21% from seasonality over the previous LSTM model variants. The interpretation here is that seasonality can be more accurately inferred for the few product segments having the largest revenues, and hence the segment-level benefits are outweighed world-wide by the many smaller-revenue datarows that are less accurate (due to more fluctuation in seasonal effects on smaller products). We suggest that seasonal trend decomposition be used only after careful consideration of the durability of financial seasonality. In our application, we only present LSTM results including seasonality since we find it beneficial conjointly with curriculum learning; experimentally, our displayed results fare better than the alternative of curriculum learning sans seasonality.

Table 1. World-wide test error reduction percentages of DNN models over previous Microsoft production baseline.

Model	Percent MAPE improvement
Basic LSTM	1.9%
LSTM with categorical indicators	18.2%
LSTM with seasonality	−5.1%
LSTM with curriculum learning	**27.0%**
Basic DCNN	−0.7%
DCNN with categorical indicators	12.1%
DCNN with curriculum learning	**22.6%**

Recall that we ran each model 30 times and took outcome averages to reduce variance. Density plots are shown for world-wide results in Figs. 6 and 7, which reflect the distribution of calculated (non-absolute) percentage error for each of the LSTM and DCNN models tested, respectively. These figures allow us to examine the extent to which curriculum learning models are less biased.

Table 2. LSTM model segment-level MAPE reduction percentages (%) over previous Microsoft production baseline (positive % corresponds to error reduction).

Segment	Basic LSTM (Model (a))	Model (a) + Categorical Indicators (Model (b))	Model(b) + Seasonality (Model (c))	Model(c) + Curriculum Learning (Model(d))
1	25.5	22.0	53.4	70.0
2	−47.9	−34.3	−23.0	−0.8
3	7.65	−5.8	26.0	20.3
4	14.2	30.3	12.0	27.4
5	−15.4	−13.2	−11.8	−25.9
6	−79.2	−60.3	−110.1	−12.4
7	34.7	30.1	31.0	11.5
8	17.9	15.5	57.2	61.4
Revenue-weighted average	**10.3**	**10.3**	**21.3**	**30.0**

For both density plots, the y-axis denoting density is fully presented. However, note that the x-axis (expressing percent error) values aside from 0 are excluded for Microsoft privacy reasons. For both LSTM and DCNN models, we can disclose that the spread of error is bounded by a range of approximately ±10 percentage points. We claim that applying curriculum learning to our DNN models lessens bias as percent errors are shifted towards zero.

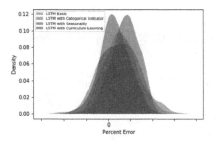
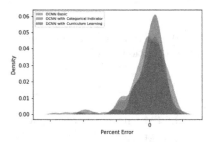

Fig. 6. LSTM world-wide error density (Color figure online)

Fig. 7. DCNN world-wide error density (Color figure online)

In Fig. 6, comparisons are displayed among the Basic LSTM (blue), LSTM with Categorical Indicator (orange), LSTM with Seasonality (green), and LSTM with Curriculum Learning (red). In Fig. 7, comparisons are displayed among the Basic DCNN (blue), DCNN with Categorical Indicator (orange), and DCNN with Curriculum Learning (green). In both cases, we see that the curriculum learning variant (red for LSTM, and green for DCNN) is both closest to being zero-centered and is one of the models with lowest variance.

5.2   Segment-Level MAPEs

In Tables 2 and 3 below, we share the segment-level incremental improvement percentages obtained from the Encoder-Decoder LSTM and DCNN model MAPEs, respectively, as compared to Microsoft's previously-implemented baseline. Due to privacy concerns, the actual names of the segments are not shared since their revenues are considered High Business Impact (HBI) data.

Overall, the revenue-weighted LSTM segment-level MAPEs show a drastic 30% improvement in MAPE relative to the Microsoft baseline currently used in production (see Table 2). This strong showing is robust both within-segment and world-wide, as seen in Table 1. Similar gains from curriculum learning are reflected in the DCNN model (see Table 3), showing a 19% point increase from the basic DCNN model to the variant with curriculum learning.

Despite the fact that we cannot discuss segment-specific results in terms of absolute numbers, we comment that it is clear that some segments see significant gains relative to the Microsoft production baseline, whereas others only see modest gains (or slight decreases). In particular, the addition of curriculum learning with our uniformly-weighted ordering improves results for larger-revenue segments. However, when using batches based on segment, and using a reverse ordering of segments from hardest to easiest to predict (based on seasonality as we have been doing; results for this variant are not disclosed in this paper), the most improvement is seen in smaller-revenue segments, which otherwise would have been overshadowed by model weights contributing towards larger-revenue segments. Thus, ensembling these two different sorts is a promising future step.

Table 3. DCNN Model Segment-level MAPE reduction percentages (%) over previous Microsoft production baseline (positive % corresponds to error reduction).

Segment	Basic DCNN (Model (a))	Model (a) + Categorical Indicators (Model (b))	Model(b) + Curriculum Learning (Model (c))
1	24.8	44.0	34.2
2	−0.2	−19.5	−19.5
3	−8.7	28.9	39.9
4	35.5	35.4	22.6
5	45.4	58.4	26.8
6	−258.2	−263.2	−80.5
7	27.0	28.7	29.4
8	33.8	35.5	24.9
Revenue-weighted average	**−3.1**	**4.5**	**16.2**

We now turn to examples of segment-specific density plots, which are shown for two specific segments in Figs. 8 through 11. For privacy reasons, we cannot disclose the segment names, but we assert that one of the segments has larger revenue, and one of the segments has smaller revenue (amounting to four times less revenue than the larger segment). In the below plots, we show both segment sizes for which curriculum learning improves results. We use these figures firstly to re-affirm the effect of curriculum learning on bias, but also to comment on across-run variance. Again, we note that the x-axis (expressing percent error) values aside from 0 are excluded for Microsoft privacy reasons.

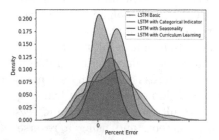

Fig. 8. LSTM larger segment error (Color figure online)

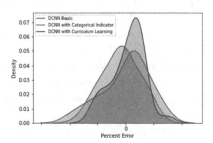

Fig. 9. DCNN larger segment error (Color figure online)

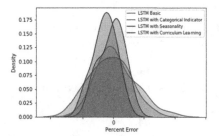

Fig. 10. LSTM smaller segment error (Color figure online)

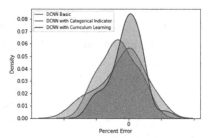

Fig. 11. DCNN smaller segment error (Color figure online)

We compare the same model variants as in the previous world-wide figures. Specifically, in Figs. 8 and 10, comparisons are displayed among the Basic LSTM (blue), LSTM with Categorical Indicator (orange), LSTM with Seasonality (green), and LSTM with Curriculum Learning (red). In Figs. 9 and 11, comparisons are displayed among the Basic DCNN (blue), DCNN with Categorical Indicator (orange), and DCNN with Curriculum Learning (green).

We first discuss the larger-revenue segment's density plots (Fig. 8 for LSTM models, and Fig. 9 for DCNN models). We find that the LSTM model with curriculum learning, in particular, improves both bias (towards zero) and variance, as the density spread is decidedly smaller than other model variants. These effects are less pronounced but similar (especially for lessening variance, but less so for improving bias) for the DCNN model with curriculum learning.

We now discuss the smaller-revenue segment's density plots (Fig. 10 for LSTM models, and Fig. 11 for DCNN models). We find that the DCNN with curriculum learning model, in particular, improves both bias (towards zero) and variance. These effects are less pronounced but similar (moreso for lessening variance) for the LSTM model with curriculum learning.

Based on the above, we see at the segment level that there can occur a bias and variance trade-off. Specifically, for the segments wherein curriculum learning improves accuracy, some will see lessened bias (with little change in variance from non-curriculum learning model variants), some will see lessened variance (with little change in bias from non-curriculum learning model variants), and some instances yield better bias and variance. Hence, we conclude that curriculum learning models on our financial time series for specific segments not only yield more accurate forecasts, but also can achieve relatively low variance and bias.

6 Discussion

It is clear from our results that there is value in using DNNs on Microsoft's financial time series, and further that curriculum learning is an indispensable tool to improve accuracy of forecasts. These curriculum learning results are robust both world-wide and at the segment-level. Further, we see from Figs. 6 and 7 that curriculum learning allows for less bias in errors (robust across both LSTM and DCNN methods), and in certain instances less variance in error at the segment level.

We return to our key methodological takeaways from our work as presented. First, curriculum learning is a powerful technique for time series data, not just in NLP problems; applying a good sorting metric to neural network batches can improve results drastically.

Second, we contribute much of the efficiency of our DNN methods to transfer learning effects, which are particularly useful for products with a relatively short revenue history. Here, it is worth noting the importance of data pre-processing. Executing our DNN methods without regard for missing data yielded worse results than when we subset to training on data with enough historical trends. Applying the latter model to datarows without sufficient history yielded good results, showing evidence of transfer learning across region, segment, and product.

Lastly, financial data do not need to be extraordinarily large to successfully use neural networks on forecasting. DNN methods are far more efficient than the Microsoft production baseline that involves ensembling traditional statistical and machine learning methods; it takes a fraction of the time spent to run each DNN model. While curriculum learning involves sorting, and hence may be unwieldy for very large datasets, it does not significantly impact runtime on the "medium-sized" Microsoft data, and we are able to create models that do not overfit the data.

Future work includes testing more metrics for curriculum learning, comparing these results to changing sample weights of the hierarchical variables, and ensembling these models for greater accuracy. It would be prudent for future hypertuning packages to include curriculum learning batch metrics and batch sizes as parameters. We hope to see greater use of DNNs in industry, in particular using curriculum learning on medium-sized datasets.

Acknowledgements. We thank Kimyen Nguyen for her generous help with running experiments on security compliant machines considering the sensitivity of the finance data. We also thank Barbara Stortz, Deependra Hamal, and Mindy Yamamoto for their support of this project. The work of A.K. is jointly supported by Microsoft and the National Science Foundation Graduate Research Fellowship under Grant No. DGE – 1656518. Any opinion, findings, and conclusions or recommendations expressed in this material are those of the authors and do not necessarily reflect the views of the National Science Foundation.

References

1. Barker, J., Gajewar, A., Golyaev, K., Bansal, G., Conners, M.: Secure and automated enterprise revenue forecasting. In: The Thirtieth AAAI Conference on Innovative Applications of Artificial Intelligence, pp. 7657–7664 (2018)
2. Bengio, Y., Louradour, J., Collobert, R., Weston, J.: Curriculum learning. In: Proceedings of the 26th Annual International Conference on Machine Learning, pp. 41–48. ACM (2009)
3. Borovykh, A., Bohte, S., Oosterlee, C.: Conditional time series forecasting with convolutional neural networks (2018)
4. Cirik, V., Hovy, E., Morency, L.P.: Visualizing and understanding curriculum learning for long short-term memory networks (2016)
5. Cleveland, R., Cleveland, W., McRae, J., Terpenning, I.: STL: a seasonal-trend decomposition procedure based on loess. J. Off. Stat. **6**(1), 3–73 (1990)
6. Gajewar, A.: Improving regional revenue forecasts using product hierarchy. In: 39th International Symposium on Forecasting (2018)
7. Graves, A., Bellemare, M.G., Menick, J., Munos, R., Kavukcuoglu, K.: Automated curriculum learning for neural networks (2017)
8. Fawaz, H.I., Forestier, G., Weber, J., Idoumghar, L., Muller, P.A.: Transfer learning for time series classification (2018)
9. Flunkert, V., Salinas, D., Gasthaus, J.: DeepAR: probabilistic forecasting with autoregressive recurrent networks CoRR abs/1704.04110, (2017)
10. Gupta, P., Malhotra, P., Vig, L., Shroff, G.: Transfer learning for clinical time series analysis using recurrent neural networks. In: Medicine and Healthcare Workshop at ACM KDD 2018 Conference (2018)
11. Laptev, N., Yosinski, J., Li, L.E., Smyl, S.: Time-series extreme event forecasting with neural networks at uber. In: ICML 2017 Time Series Workshop, Sydney, Australia (2017)
12. Sirignano, J., Cont, R.: Universal features of price formation in financial markets: perspectives from deep learning (2018)

13. Spitkovsky, V.I., Alshawi, H., Jurafsky, D.: From babysteps to leapfrog: how less is more in unsupervised dependency parsing. In: Human Language Technologies: The 2010 Annual Conference of the North American Chapter of the Association for Computational Linguistics, pp. 751–759. Association for Computational Linguistics (2010)
14. Sutskever, I., Vinyals, O., Le, Q.V.: Sequence to sequence learning with neural networks. In: Advances in Neural Information Processing Systems, vol. 27, pp. 3104–3112. Curran Associates, Inc. (2014)
15. Talagala, A., Hyndman, R., Athanasopoulos, G.: Meta-learning how to forecast time series. Monash Econometrics and Business Statistics Working Papers (2018)
16. Time Series Prediction with LSTM Recurrent Neural Networks in Python with Keras. https://machinelearningmastery.com/time-series-prediction-lstm-recurrent -neural-networks-python-keras. Accessed 19 Mar 2019
17. TimeSeries Seq2Seq. https://github.com/JEddy92/TimeSeries_Seq2Seq. Accessed 19 Mar 2019
18. van den OordSander, A., et al.: WaveNet: a generative model for raw audio (2016)

Representation Learning in Graphs for Credit Card Fraud Detection

Rafaël Van Belle[⊠], Sandra Mitrović, and Jochen De Weerdt

Research Center for Information Systems Engineering, KU Leuven,
Naamsestraat 69, 3000 Leuven, Belgium
rafael.vanbelle@kuleuven.be

Abstract. Representation learning in graphs has proven useful for many predictive tasks. In this paper we assess the feasibility of representation learning in a credit card fraud setting. Data analytics has been successful in predicting fraud in previous research. However, the research field has focused on techniques which require tedious and expensive hand-crafting of features. In addition, existing works often ignore information related to the network of transactions. Representation learning in graphs tackles both of these challenges. First, it provides the possibility to tap into the relational and structural aspects of the transaction network and leverage these in a predictive model. Second, it featurizes the graph without the need for manual feature engineering. This work contributes to the literature by being the first to explicitly and extensively show how fraud detection modeling can benefit from representation learning. We discern three different approaches in this paper: traditional network featurization, an inductive representation learning algorithm and a transductive representational learner. Through extensive experimental evaluation on a real-world dataset we show that state-of-the-art representation learning in graphs outperforms traditional graph featurization.

1 Introduction

In an increasingly cash-less society [9], the importance of transaction fraud detection cannot be underestimated. In the case of credit card transactions, every transaction leaves a data trail which can help to identify fraudulent transactions before they are authorised. The combination of this transaction data with recent machine learning (ML) techniques has enabled the automatic identification of fraudulent transactions. While many researchers have developed and applied machine learning algorithms for fraud detection [2,6,16,20,24,26], they often depend on hand-crafted feature engineering which is tedious, case-dependent and difficult to optimize. In addition, despite the fact that recent research has shown that fraudulent behavior has an important social effect, both the social as well as the temporal aspect of fraudulent behavior is often ignored [28].

Representation learning is a set of techniques that are capable of learning task-independent, dense vectors or embeddings for objects of interest [4]. The techniques were first developed in the context of natural language processing

© Springer Nature Switzerland AG 2020
V. Bitetta et al. (Eds.): MIDAS 2019, LNAI 11985, pp. 32–46, 2020.
https://doi.org/10.1007/978-3-030-37720-5_3

(NLP), however they have been extended to other types of data such as images and networks. As such, node embedding is one representation learning technique which tries to create a low-dimensional, continuous latent vector representation for each node in a graph [10]. This vector, in turn, preserves the relational structure of the graph. The goal is to derive a general-purpose representation of nodes in a graph that can enable performant applications of machine learning techniques for downstream tasks, including for instance node classification.

In this paper, we scrutinize how representation learning can improve automated, ML-based fraud detection. Despite the abundance of node embedding algorithms available, most existing methods are unadapted in different ways for fraud detection. For instance, node embedding techniques are often transductive, which implies all nodes need to be present in the network from the start. Thus, the embeddings cannot be generalised to unseen nodes. While credit card transactions arrive continuously, adding nodes to the network over time, requires to come up with new embeddings, without time for retraining.

Accordingly, this paper puts forward the following contributions:

- This study is the first to explicitly show the added value of representation learning for (credit card) fraud detection in an empirical investigation using a real-life transaction dataset containing over three million transactions. Our experimental design addresses the extreme class imbalance and timeliness constraints.
- We analyze the impact of altering the default network architecture by introducing artificial nodes in the network.
- We assess the feasibility of expanding existing transductive representational learners such that they work incrementally without full retraining.

The remainder of the paper is structured as follows. First, we provide an overview of related work. Next, in Sect. 3 we introduce both the traditional graph featurization technique and the representation learning algorithms used in this paper. Subsequently Sect. 4 details the extensive experimental analysis, with the results presented in the next section. Section 6 concludes the paper.

2   Related Work

This study is related to a varied set of topics. We provide a brief overview of machine learning techniques for fraud detection, the use of social network data, representation learning in graphs, and the associated inductive problem.

Machine Learning for Fraud Detection. In the last decade, the number of credit card transactions has increased significantly, giving rise to the need of more automated, data-driven fraud detection.

Machine learning techniques for fraud detection can be categorized as either supervised or unsupervised. On the one hand, unsupervised methods seek to detect deviations from behavioral patterns [6,20,23,26,29].

On the other hand, supervised fraud detection starts from a labeled dataset containing transactions which are known to either be genuine or fraudulent. A study by [5] applied traditional supervised classifiers, such as logistic regression and support vector machines.

More recently ensemble learners and hybrid approaches are becoming more prevalent, such as Random forests [24,31]. Similarly, the authors of [1] studied bagging with Bayesian inference-based learners.

Furthermore, a considerable amount of research has focused on neural networks for fraud detection [2,15,16].

Machine learning for fraud detection faces several challenges. First, fraud is inherently dynamic given that fraudsters quickly adapt to new detection techniques [24,25]. Furthermore, at the data level, extremely skewed data sets pose a significant challenge for producing high-quality detection models [1]. Third, baseline performance of these models needs to be high, given that both false positives as well as false negatives are usually very undesired.

Social Network-Driven Fraud Detection. Fraudulent behavior has an important social dimension. [28] is among the first to explicitly consider the relational aspects of fraud. The authors apply a personalized Pagerank algorithm on top of the credit card transaction network. The Pagerank algorithm is a collective inference method, which yields suspicion scores for every node in a graph. The suspicion is the result of spreading the influences of confirmed fraudulent transaction nodes across the network. However, leveraging relational information still requires hand-crafted features, just like much of the research discussed so far depends heavily on extensive feature engineering [3]. Given the diversity in fraud behavior and its dynamic nature, a solution for fraud detection without constructing tailor-made features would be valuable.

Representation Learning in Graphs. The key challenge in using graphs in machine learning is transforming them into a format which can be incorporated into a machine learning model while preserving as much structural information as possible [12]. Traditional approaches employ hand-crafted features based on graph statistics (e.g. node degree) or kernel functions, leaving a substantial part of structural information uncaptured.

More recent research has tackled this challenge in many different ways, introducing techniques like graph neural networks and matrix factorization [7,13,27]. A recent representation technique was inspired by the field of Natural Language Processing (NLP) where neural language models use the context information in sentences to predict target words [17]. In [19], the authors introduced DeepWalk, which applies the idea from NLP to graphs, rather than text. Words are replaced by nodes and node sequences serve as replacement for sentences. Through optimization DeepWalk provides latent vector representations for each node in the network.

Inductive Representation Learning. Recently scholars introduced inductive representation learners. Graphsage [12], for instance, is an inductive node embedding framework that leverages local node neighborhood feature information. The algorithm learns a function to generate new embeddings for unseen nodes. While

Graphsage was initially conceived for graphs with rich node attributes, the algorithm can deal with graphs without node features [12].

The approach used in [22] is similar to the idea in Graphsage, i.e. a graph convolutional neural network which aggregates k-hop local feature information in a hierarchical manner. By contrast, in [14] inductive representation learning is achieved via incremental singular value decomposition.

Aforementioned techniques have a considerable complexity and computational burden. Hence, in this study more intuitive inductive operators are tested on shallow node embeddings (instead of deep neural network architectures). This idea of inductive shallow node embedding has been pursued by other researchers. SPINE [11], for instance, combines Pagerank with the SkipGram model and captures both local proximity and proximity at any distance, which allows for improved structural identity identification. Inductive representation learning has already been applied for fraud detection [30, 32]. However, this study starts from a graph with a small set of node features and our experiments focus on supervised learning rather than unsupervised as in [32].

3   Inductive Representation Learning-Based Fraud Detection

This section details the building blocks for applying representation learning in a fraud detection setting. First, the relational structure is explicitly encoded into a graph format. Then, every graph vertex is transformed into a vector by means of a representation learning algorithm. Generalizing these embeddings to unseen nodes is achieved with the help of an inductive extension, which is introduced at the end of the section.

3.1   Graph Structure

The simplest networks consist of a single node type. Transaction networks, in contrast, contain two distinctive types of entities: cardholders and merchants. Transactions can be represented as edges connecting merchants and cardholders. However, in this paper we followed the approach described in [28] to represent every transaction as a vertex as well. This increases the network complexity, but at the same time increases the opportunities for inductive operators because in addition to embeddings for merchants and cardholders, every transaction can be encoded in a separate embedding. Figure 1 illustrates the bipartite vs. tripartite graph structures.

Artificially augmenting this graph architecture by for instance, adding an artificial node associated to the previously known members of the positive class [18] can potentially benefit the subsequent representation learning (see Fig. 1). This idea is also relevant for fraud detection, as it seems interesting to explicitly add historical fraud information to the network data, e.g. to resemble spreading activation-based techniques such as Pagerank. In the experimental evaluation,

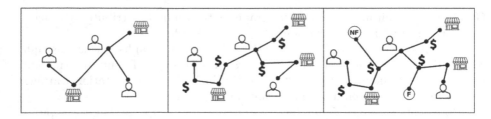

Fig. 1. Left: bipartite graph with cardholders and merchants connected through edges representing transactions. Middle: tripartite graph with transactions transformed into nodes (dollar signs). Right: artificial 'fraud' (F) and 'non-fraud' (NF) nodes join the graph and are connected to historical transactions with known labels.

we will therefore assess the addition of two artificial nodes to which we connect all fraudulent transactions and all non-fraudulent transactions respectively ('Pooling+').

3.2   Traditional Network Featurization

The transformation of a graph into a usable format for machine learning can be achieved in many ways. One approach is to summarize the graph through a number of network related metrics. Node degree, betweenness and closeness are examples of metrics capturing essential characteristics of the network under scrutiny.

In line with [28] we use the personalized Pagerank algorithm in our experiments. Essentially this algorithm is a spreading activation function which disseminates the fraudulent behavior from confirmed, historical fraud cases to neighbouring nodes. Through iteration the fraudulent influences spread further into the network until a point of convergence is reached. The result is a suspicion score for each node in the network. This score can then be leveraged by downstream predictive algorithms.

3.3   Transductive Representation Learning

The main objective of this work is to compare the performance of graph representation learning algorithms against the traditional approach of graph featurization, in this case, suspicion scores based on personalized Pagerank. To this end we consider two representational learners: Graphsage (see Sect. 2), which is inherently inductive and a transductive representational learner based on well-known Node2vec [10].

Similar to a notable number of representation learning approaches, including Node2vec, our approach consists of two steps: the generation of random walks and the learning of node representations based on the obtained random walks using SkipGram model [17]. Node2vec claims to outperform other node representation learning methods due to flexible random walks obtained by introducing two additional parameters (return parameter p and in-out parameter q). However, this flexibility leads to a high computational cost. Furthermore, there are no clear guidelines on determining the most optimal values for these parameters. Therefore, in line with [18], we opt for discarding these additional parameters and, instead, considering purely (but still truncated) random walks.

Once random walks are generated, SkipGram model is applied, aiming at maximizing the posterior probability of node co-occurrence, that is, for any arbitrarily chosen node v:

$$\max_{f} \prod_{c \in C_v} Pr(f(c)|f(v))$$

where C_v is a context of node v defined by a random walk and f is a targeted mapping function to be learnt. This conditional probability is modelled using a softmax function, leading to the following objective function:

$$\max_{f} \sum_{v \in V} \sum_{c \in C_v} \left(f(c) \cdot f(v) - log \sum_{c' \in C} e^{f(c') \cdot f(v)} \right)$$

which is further simplified using negative sampling, with five negative samples as suggested by [17].

3.4 From Transductive Towards Inductive Representation Learning

The need for inductive representation learning can be related to the timeliness constraints in many application domains. Fraud detection is no exception. When a transaction is processed, authorization is required in a matter of seconds. As discussed before, existing representation learning techniques are mainly transductive (see Sect. 2). The entire graph is only fed once to the representational learner, which only produces a single batch of embeddings. Adding or removing nodes or edges to the network, requires re-iterating the entire process. The associated computational complexity impedes the timely completion of the prediction.

Graphsage [12] is a node embedding algorithm capable of generating embeddings for unseen nodes. Hence, this technique is an obvious choice to tackle the induction problem for fraud. Graphsage circumvents iterations by learning functions which use neighbourhood node attributes as input and generate embeddings as output. Graphsage offers an array of possibilities for feature aggregations to apply on the node attributes. Our choice for neighborhood feature aggregators was based on the results in [12], where maxpool and meanpool aggregators delivered the best results.

In this section, we also aim to investigate the extension of transductive representational learners (see Sect. 3.3), like Node2vec, to generate inductive node embeddings. We describe a simple procedure to create embeddings for unseen nodes, i.e. a new credit card transaction. The underlying idea is to run the embedding algorithm on a sufficient amount of training data. For every new graph element which is added to the original graph, a new embedding is created by reusing embeddings already derived for existing graph elements (see Fig. 2).

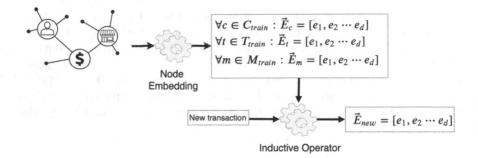

$$\forall c \in C_{train} : \vec{E}_c = [e_1, e_2 \cdots e_d]$$
$$\forall t \in T_{train} : \vec{E}_t = [e_1, e_2 \cdots e_d]$$
$$\forall m \in M_{train} : \vec{E}_m = [e_1, e_2 \cdots e_d]$$

Node Embedding

New transaction

$$\vec{E}_{new} = [e_1, e_2 \cdots e_d]$$

Inductive Operator

Fig. 2. High-level overview of inductive node embedding. Each node is encoded into a vector E with a node embedding algorithm. When a new transaction arrives, an inductive operator is applied, using information from the original embeddings (E_c, E_t, E_m) to yield a unique embedding E_{new} for the new transaction. C_{train} is the set of cardholders in the training data, E_c is a cardholder embedding. The same reasoning applies to transactions (T_{train}) and merchants (M_{train}). d is the dimension of the embedding vector.

Pooling. The inductive extension needs to handle four scenarios upon arrival of a new transaction. First scenario: the merchant and cardholder have never been seen before, which implies there is no link to any historical embedding. In this case the induced embedding will be based on an overall average of all other embeddings. The second and third scenario occur when respectively the merchant or the cardholder has executed one or more transactions before. The new transaction embedding will use a copy of the merchant or cardholder embedding respectively. Finally, in scenario four, both merchant and cardholder may already be present in the transaction network. In this case, both have already been encoded into a vector representation (embedding) as well as the transactions between them. In this last scenario, we simply compute the average of the embeddings of the cardholder and merchant.

4 Experimental Setup

4.1 Dataset

Summary statistics concerning the data are listed in Table 1, with Table 2 containing a small excerpt to illustrate the dataset structure.

Preprocessing of the dataset consists of two steps. First, all transactions which failed due to other reasons than fraud where discarded from the dataset (e.g. wrong PIN code), and secondly some outliers were removed, mainly transactions above 5,000 EUR.

Figure 3 depicts the partitioning of data into five independent subsets. Each subset is additionally split into a training (4 days) and test set (1 day). Each experiment is repeated five times, once for every subset, which delivered valuable insights regarding the robustness of predictive performance.

Table 1. Summary statistics

Number of entries	3,240,339
Start date	01-10-2013
End date	06-11-2013
Unique cardholders	1,240,216
Unique merchants	129,814
Fraudulent transactions	12,618
Genuine transactions	3,227,721
Fraud rate	0.38%

Table 2. Excerpt from the credit card fraud dataset used in this paper. Each line represents one transaction and contains identifiers of parties involved (Cardholder, Merchant) along with timestamp information (Timestamp) and monetary amount of the transaction (Amount). In addition, the country of the Merchant (Country) and Merchant category are reported (Cat.).

TX	Cardholder	Merchant	Cat.	Country	Amount	Timestamp	Fraud
t0	AC83FD	m000174	4816	USA	7.37	2013-10-01 01:00:06	False
t1	1CD10E	m207001	5735	LUX	6.25	2013-10-01 01:00:08	False
t2	4ECA55	m003020	7523	CAN	7.18	2013-10-01 01:00:08	False
t3	74186F	m800002	4812	USA	154.93	2013-10-01 01:00:09	True
t4	8777F3	m000102	7399	BEL	15.00	2013-10-01 01:00:10	False

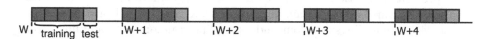

Fig. 3. Five weeks of data are divided in five independent subsets, which in turn are subdivided into a training (green) and test set (red). (Color figure online)

4.2 Tools

The majority of experiments are executed with Python. The Pagerank algorithm is implemented based on the description in [28]. The experiments with Graphsage are executed with the implementation made available by the authors of [12]. Finally, the remainder of experiments is based on a modified version of the Node2Vec algorithm [10] proposed by the authors of [18]. This algorithm consists of two parts: random walk generator and Skipgram model (see Sect. 3). The random walking algorithm had to be re-implemented in C++ due to the size of our networks. We found the existing implementations to be memory-inefficient and slow. For the second part, i.e. the Skipgram model, the implementation in [21] was used. All experiments were executed with 32 virtual CPUs (Intel Haswell) and 32 GB of memory (Table 3).

Table 3. Statistics of the five datasets used for training. Notation: $|V|$ number of nodes, $|E|$ number of edges, $|C|$ number of cardholders, $|M|$ number of merchants, $|T|$ number of transactions.

	W (set 1)	W+1 (set 2)	W+2 (set 3)	W+3 (set 4)	W+4 (set 5)
$|V|$	634,826	649,028	645,984	643,990	633,201
$|E|$	691,776	709,294	710,384	706,550	688,426
$|C|$	255,848	262,115	259,853	258,421	256,136
$|M|$	33,090	32,266	30,939	32,294	32,852
$|T|$	345,888	354,647	355,192	353,275	344,213
Fraud rate	0.57%	0.41%	0.23%	0.20%	0.28%

4.3   Experimental Design

The experimental design consists of two factors which yield a total of 16 settings to test on 5 featurization algorithms (see Sects. 3.2 and 3.4).

– **Sampling:** random undersampling, random oversampling, SMOTE, ADASYN.
– **Predictive learner:** logistic regression, SVM, XGBoost, random forest.
– **Featurization technique:** Pagerank, Graphsage with meanpool, Graphsage with maxpool, Pooling without artificial nodes ('pooling−'), Pooling with artificial nodes ('pooling+')

As previously mentioned, credit card fraud data suffers from a severe class imbalance. To this end, four sampling approaches are applied on the training dataset with embeddings: random undersampling, random oversampling, oversampling with SMOTE and oversampling with ADASYN. The sampling procedure always aims for a 40/60 distribution of fraud/non-fraud labels in the final dataset.

Second factor is the predictive algorithm. Logistic regression is used de facto in many works on representation learning [10,18]. Moreover, the experiments are repeated with Support Vector Machines (SVM), which are known to perform well on high-dimensional data. eXtreme Gradient Boosting (XGBoost) and Random Forest (RF) are two ensemble learners which conclude the list of predictive algorithms.

The personalized Pagerank algorithm from [28] will be used as benchmark. For the purpose of this paper the setup in [28] is replicated, which implies running the algorithm for three different hyperparameter sets. The single hyperparameter of Pagerank influences how far the fraud can spread before reaching convergence. All three suspicion scores are combined and used for the machine learning phase.

So far, all details regarding the experimental evaluation have been discussed. However, the representational learner responsible for the embeddings in the training dataset also has a number of hyperparameters (see Sect. 3.3). The choice for these hyperparameters is a trade-off in terms of expressiveness and computational burden. They are fixed across all experiments. The dimension of embeddings is set at 32, number of nodes in a walk is 20 and number of walks for each node is 10. Default values are used for parameters related to the Skipgram model [17].

4.4 Evaluation Metrics

For comparison among algorithms the average AUC score of five independent replications will be reported. The AUC score is highly resilient to the class imbalance present in fraud data. In addition, the F1-score is reported to take into account the precision/recall trade-off, which might not be obvious from an AUC score alone. Finally, Lift at 10% is used to take into account the limited resource availability within the industry for inspection of fraud cases.

5 Results

Overall results. To compare the differences between the algorithms, Fig. 4 depicts the AUC scores for each technique across all sixteen scenarios. Table 4 contains the average scores across these sixteen settings which were each replicated five times (see Sect. 4).

A first look reveals encouraging results for the pooling inductive operators. Both perform almost equally well on AUC measure, while the 'Pooling+' operator clearly outperforms 'Pooling-' in terms of F1-score and lift. These results illustrate the potential for adding artificial nodes into the network ('Pooling+' contains two artificial nodes, see Sect. 3.1). It is apparent from this table that both pooling operators perform considerably better than the Pagerank baseline algorithm in terms of AUC and lift at 10%. What is particularly striking is the performance of the Pooling operators outperforming Graphsage with meanpool operator in respect of AUC, F1-score and lift. The other variant of Graphsage with maxpool operator performs on par with respect to the pooling operators. Overall, these results show that our pooling operators can match and even outperform state-of-the-art baseline algorithms.

If we now turn to the *'max'* columns of Table 4, it becomes apparent that performance of most pooling operators can be further increased, provided that the combination of sampling strategy and predictive algorithm is chosen carefully.

Next, a non-parametric Friedman test with the extension by Iman and Davenport [8] is applied to assess whether there is a statistically significant difference in performance. For that, the AUC, F1 and lift scores are 'blocked' according to the combinations of sampling strategy and classifier in order to avoid confounding effects. The Friedman test rejects the null-hypothesis (p-value: < 0.01) which implies not all techniques perform the same, regardless of the metric.

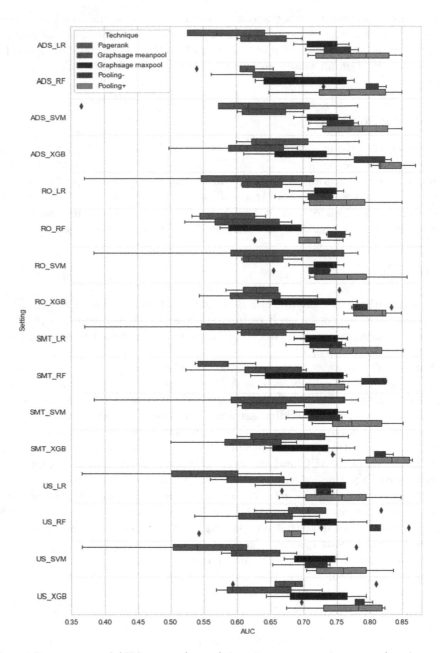

Fig. 4. Comparison of AUC scores (x-axis) for all experimental settings (combination of sampling strategy and classifier)(y-axis). Each boxplot shows the result from 5 independent replications. **Notation:** ADS - ADASYN oversampling, RO - random oversampling, SMT - SMOTE oversampling, US - undersampling, LR - logistic regression, RF - random forests, XGB - XGBoost.

Table 4. Comparison of techniques in terms of AUC, F1 score and lift at 10%. For each performance measure the average ± standard deviation is reported alongside the maximum performance. The average (avg) is calculated based on five replications for each of the 16 settings. The reported maximum (max) is an average of five replications of one particular choice of factor settings (one of the 16 possible settings). Best results for each metric have been underlined. **Notation**: 'pooling−', pooling without artificial nodes, 'pooling+', pooling with artificial nodes

Technique	AUC		F1		Lift	
	avg	max	avg	max	avg	max
Pagerank	0.62 ± 0.10	0.71	0.16 ± 0.08	0.39	1.25 ± 0.56	2.66
Graphsage meanpool	0.63 ± 0.05	0.64	0.04 ± 0.05	0.10	2.01 ± 0.84	2.59
Graphsage maxpool	0.71 ± 0.05	0.73	0.05 ± 0.05	0.13	2.76 ± 0.97	3.82
Pooling−	0.76 ± 0.03	0.80	0.05 ± 0.05	0.23	2.91 ± 0.93	4.89
Pooling+	0.77 ± 0.04	0.83	0.18 ± 0.12	0.40	3.83 ± 0.57	4.53

Pairwise Comparisons. In the end, a post-hoc Nemenyi test is applied to assess statistically significant differences in AUC scores among particular combinations of sampling strategy, feature engineering technique (Pagerank, Graphsage, Pooling...) and classifiers. This post-hoc procedure corrects for multiple hypothesis testing and controls the family-wise error rate [8]. In total, 80 configurations are compared in a pairwise fashion. A limited number of tests exceeded the critical value associated with the Nemenyi test (Critical value: 62.50).

In Table 5 a selection of significant results is presented. It clearly shows that Pagerank and Graphsage meanpool are the only techniques which are statistically significantly worse. Most striking is the fact that XGBoost and oversampling are used by all configurations which are significantly better than others. Next to this, only the pooling operator seems to outperform the Pagerank algorithm and Graphsage meanpool, while for Graphsage maxpool no such conclusion can be reached.

Runtime. The personalized Pagerank algorithm ran in 9'3". Creation of embeddings took on average 7'29" and 28'46" with respectively Pooling and Graphsage. Average prediction runtime amounted to 9'13" (XGBoost) (measured on first week dataset).

Table 5. Selection of results from the Nemenyi test for pairwise comparisons. The 'weaker' configurations are reported in the left side column, while 'stronger' options are shown in the top row. Numbers in bold exceed the critical value for the Nemenyi test, which implies that the configuration in the top row is significantly better than the configuration in the left hand column.

Technique + Sampling + Classifier	pooling− RO XGB	pooling+ RO XGB	pooling+ SMT XGB	pooling+ ADS XGB
Pagerank US SVM	56.6	59.4	61.6	**63.0**
Pagerank US LR	62.2	**65.0**	**67.2**	68.6
Pagerank ADS LR	59.8	**62.6**	**64.8**	66.2
Pagerank RO RF	**62.7**	**65.5**	**67.7**	69.1
Pagerank SMOTE RF	**63.3**	**66.1**	**68.3**	69.7
Graphsage meanpool RO RF	58.0	60.8	**63.0**	64.4
Graphsage meanpool US LR	56.6	59.4	61.6	**63.0**
Graphsage meanpool SMT XGB	56.2	59.0	61.2	**62.6**

6   Conclusion

The major objective of this work was to assess the feasibility for graph representation learning in a credit card fraud detection setting. State-of-the art (inductive) representation learning techniques were compared against a traditional approach for graph featurization (Pagerank). Furthermore, we demonstrated the benefits of introducing artificial nodes in the network ('pooling+'). We also introduced inductive operators for existing transductive representational learners (i.e. Node2vec) and illustrated their on par performance with state-of-the-art inductive algorithms (i.e Graphsage).

From the obtained results, we can conclude that simple inductive operators exemplify the *keep it simple* principle. The relatively poor performance of the Graphsage technique should be further explored as well, however no other relevant experimental comparisons of Graphsage with other inductive strategies were found in the literature that could challenge or confirm our findings.

Further research might explore the effect of random walks with explicit consideration of node type heterogeneity. In addition, theoretically underpinning the empirically measured effect of artificial nodes in graphs would be useful. Finally, this study can be extended with financial performance measures, which take profit and loss considerations into account explicitly.

Acknowledgement. We acknowledge the support given by the Research Fund - Flanders (FWO) as Aspirant (Rafaël Van Belle).

References

1. Akila, S., Reddy, U.S.: Cost-sensitive risk induced Bayesian inference bagging (RIBIB) for credit card fraud detection. J. Comput. Sci. **27**, 247–254 (2018)
2. Aleskerov, E., Freisleben, B., Rao, B.: CARDWATCH: a neural network based database mining system for credit card fraud detection. In: Proceedings of the IEEE/IAFE 1997 Computational Intelligence for Financial Engineering (CIFEr), pp. 220–226. IEEE (1997)
3. Bahnsen, A.C., Aouada, D., Stojanovic, A., Ottersten, B.: Feature engineering strategies for credit card fraud detection. Expert Syst. Appl. **51**, 134–142 (2016)
4. Bengio, Y., Courville, A., Vincent, P.: Representation learning: a review and new perspectives. IEEE Trans. Pattern Anal. Mach. Intell. **35**(8), 1798–1828 (2013)
5. Bhattacharyya, S., Jha, S., Tharakunnel, K., Westland, J.C.: Data mining for credit card fraud: a comparative study. Decis. Support Syst. **50**(3), 602–613 (2011)
6. Bolton, R.J., Hand, D.J., et al.: Unsupervised profiling methods for fraud detection. Credit Scoring and Credit Control VII, 235–255 (2001)
7. Cao, S., Lu, W., Xu, Q.: GraRep: learning graph representations with global structural information. In: Proceedings of the 24th ACM International on Conference on Information and Knowledge Management, pp. 891–900. ACM (2015)
8. Demšar, J.: Statistical comparisons of classifiers over multiple data sets. J. Mach. Learn. Res. **7**(Jan), 1–30 (2006)
9. Fabris, N.: Cashless society-the future of money or a Utopia? J. Cent. Bank. Theory Pract. **8**(1), 53–66 (2019)
10. Grover, A., Leskovec, J.: node2vec: scalable feature learning for networks. In: Proceedings of the 22nd ACM SIGKDD International Conference on Knowledge Discovery and Data Mining, pp. 855–864. ACM (2016)
11. Guo, J., Xu, L., Chen, E.: Spine: structural identity preserved inductive network embedding. arXiv preprint arXiv:1802.03984 (2018)
12. Hamilton, W., Ying, Z., Leskovec, J.: Inductive representation learning on large graphs. In: Advances in Neural Information Processing Systems, pp. 1024–1034 (2017)
13. Hamilton, W.L., Ying, R., Leskovec, J.: Representation learning on graphs: methods and applications. CoRR abs/1709.05584 (2017)
14. Jiang, F., Zheng, L., Xu, J., Yu, P.: Fi-grl: Fast inductive graph representation learning via projection-cost preservation. In: 2018 IEEE International Conference on Data Mining (ICDM), pp. 1067–1072. IEEE (2018)
15. Jurgovsky, J., et al.: Sequence classification for credit-card fraud detection. Expert Syst. Appl. **100**, 234–245 (2018)
16. Maes, S., Tuyls, K., Vanschoenwinkel, B., Manderick, B.: Credit card fraud detection using Bayesian and neural networks. In: Proceedings of the 1st International Naiso Congress on Neuro Fuzzy Technologies, pp. 261–270 (2002)
17. Mikolov, T., Sutskever, I., Chen, K., Corrado, G.S., Dean, J.: Distributed representations of words and phrases and their compositionality. In: Advances in Neural Information Processing Systems, pp. 3111–3119 (2013)
18. Mitrović, S., Baesens, B., Lemahieu, W., De Weerdt, J.: tcc2vec: RFM-informed representation learning on call graphs for churn prediction. Inf. Sci. (2019). https://doi.org/10.1016/j.ins.2019.02.044
19. Perozzi, B., Al-Rfou, R., Skiena, S.: DeepWalk: online learning of social representations. In: Proceedings of the 20th ACM SIGKDD International Conference on Knowledge Discovery and Data Mining, pp. 701–710. ACM (2014)

20. Porwal, U., Mukund, S.: Credit card fraud detection in e-commerce: an outlier detection approach. arXiv preprint arXiv:1811.02196 (2018)
21. Řehůřek, R., Sojka, P.: Software framework for topic modelling with large corpora. In: Proceedings of the LREC 2010 Workshop on New Challenges for NLP Frameworks, pp. 45–50. ELRA (2010)
22. Rossi, R.A., Zhou, R., Ahmed, N.K.: Deep inductive network representation learning. In: Companion of the the Web Conference 2018 on the Web Conference 2018, pp. 953–960. International World Wide Web Conferences Steering Committee (2018)
23. Sánchez, D., Vila, M., Cerda, L., Serrano, J.M.: Association rules applied to credit card fraud detection. Expert Syst. Appl. 36(2), 3630–3640 (2009)
24. Sohony, I., Pratap, R., Nambiar, U.: Ensemble learning for credit card fraud detection. In: Proceedings of the ACM India Joint International Conference on Data Science and Management of Data, pp. 289–294. ACM (2018)
25. Somasundaram, A., Reddy, S.: Parallel and incremental credit card fraud detection model to handle concept drift and data imbalance. Neural Comput. Appl. 31, 1–12 (2018)
26. Srivastava, A., Kundu, A., Sural, S., Majumdar, A.: Credit card fraud detection using hidden Markov model. IEEE Trans. Dependable Secure Comput. 5(1), 37–48 (2008)
27. Tang, J., Qu, M., Wang, M., Zhang, M., Yan, J., Mei, Q.: Line: large-scale information network embedding. In: Proceedings of the 24th International Conference on World Wide Web, pp. 1067–1077. International World Wide Web Conferences Steering Committee (2015)
28. Van Vlasselaer, V., et al.: APATE: a novel approach for automated credit card transaction fraud detection using network-based extensions. Decis. Support Syst. 75, 38–48 (2015)
29. Weston, D.J., Hand, D.J., Adams, N.M., Whitrow, C., Juszczak, P.: Plastic card fraud detection using peer group analysis. Adv. Data Anal. Classif. 2(1), 45–62 (2008)
30. Xu, C., Feng, Z., Chen, Y., Wang, M., Wei, T.: FeatNet: large-scale fraud device detection by network representation learning with rich features. In: Proceedings of the 11th ACM Workshop on Artificial Intelligence and Security, pp. 57–63. ACM (2018)
31. Xuan, S., Liu, G., Li, Z., Zheng, L., Wang, S., Jiang, C.: Random forest for credit card fraud detection. In: 2018 IEEE 15th International Conference on Networking, Sensing and Control (ICNSC), pp. 1–6. IEEE (2018)
32. Yu, W., Cheng, W., Aggarwal, C.C., Zhang, K., Chen, H., Wang, W.: NetWalk: a flexible deep embedding approach for anomaly detection in dynamic networks. In: Proceedings of the 24th ACM SIGKDD International Conference on Knowledge Discovery & Data Mining, pp. 2672–2681. ACM (2018)

Firms Default Prediction with Machine Learning

Tesi Aliaj[1], Aris Anagnostopoulos[1], and Stefano Piersanti[1,2(✉)]

[1] Sapienza University of Rome, Rome, Italy
tess.aliaj@gmail.com, {aris,piersanti}@diag.uniroma1.it
[2] Bank of Italy - Statistical Data Collection and Processing Directorate, Rome, Italy

Abstract. Academics and practitioners have studied over the years models for predicting firms bankruptcy, using statistical and machine-learning approaches. An earlier sign that a company has financial difficulties and may eventually bankrupt is going in *default*, which, loosely speaking means that the company has been having difficulties in repaying its loans towards the banking system. Firms default status is not technically a failure but is very relevant for bank lending policies and often anticipates the failure of the company. Our study uses, for the first time according to our knowledge, a very large database of granular credit data from the Italian Central Credit Register of Bank of Italy that contain information on all Italian companies' past behavior towards the entire Italian banking system to predict their default using machine-learning techniques. Furthermore, we combine these data with other information regarding companies' public balance sheet data. We find that ensemble techniques and random forest provide the best results, corroborating the findings of Barboza et al. (Expert Syst. Appl., 2017).

1 Introduction

Bankruptcy prediction of a company is, not surprisingly, a topic that has attracted a lot of research in the past decades by multiple disciplines [2,4–6,8–11,13–15,19,20,22,23]. Probably the main importance of such research is in bank lending. Banks need to predict the possibility of default of a potential counterparty before they extend a loan. An effective predictive system can lead to a sounder and profitable lending decisions leading to significant savings for the banks and the companies and, most importantly, to a stable financial banking system. A stable and effective banking system is crucial for financial stability and economic recovery as well highlighted by the recent global financial crisis and European debt crisis. According to Fabio Panetta, general director of the Bank of Italy, referring to Italian loans, "The growth of the new deteriorated bank loans and the slowness of the judicial recovery procedures have determined

A. Anagnostopoulos—Partially supported by ERC Advanced Grant 788893 AMDR OMA "Algorithmic and Mechanism Design Research in Online Markets.".

V. Bitetta et al. (Eds.): MIDAS 2019, LNAI 11985, pp. 47–59, 2020.
https://doi.org/10.1007/978-3-030-37720-5_4

a rapid increase in the stock of these assets, which in 2015 reached a peak of 200 billion, equal to 11% of total loans."[1]

Of course, despite the plethora of studies, predicting the failure of a company is a hard task, as demonstrated by the large number of approaches used over time and the results of prediction still not certainly excellent.

Most related research has focused on *bankruptcy* prediction, which takes place when the company officially has the status of being unable to pay its debts (see Sect. 3). However, companies often signal much earlier their financial problems towards the banking system by going in *default*. Informally speaking, a company enters into a default state if it has failed to meet its requirement to repay its loans to the banks and it is very probable that it will not be able to meet his financial commitments in the future (again, see Sect. 3). Entering into a default state is a strong signal of a company's failure: typically banks do not finance a company into such a state and it is correlated with future bankruptcy.

Firms bankruptcy prediction and more generally creditworthiness assessment of the companies can be very important also in *policy decisions*, such as for example the policies of assignement of public guarantee programs [3].

In this paper we use historic data for predicting whether a company will enter in default. We base our analysis on two sets of data. First, we use historic information from *all the loans* obtained by *almost all the companies* based in Italy (totaling to around $800K$ companies). This information includes information on the companies credit dynamics in the past years, as well as past information on relations with banks and on values of protections associated to loans. Second, we combine these data with the balance sheets of $300K$ of these companies (the rest of them are not obliged to produce balance sheets). We apply multiple machine-learning techniques, showing that the future default status can be predicted with reasonable accuracy. Note that the dimensions and the information in our dataset exceeds significantly those of past work [4,5], allowing to obtain a very accurate picture of the possibility to predict over various economic sectors.

Contributions. To summarize the contributions of our paper are:

1. We analyze a very large dataset ($800K$ companies) with highly granular data on the performance of each company over a period of 10 year. To our knowledge, this is the most extensive dataset used in the literature.
2. We use these data to predict whether a company will default in the next year.
3. We combine our data with data available from company balance sheets, showing that we can improve further the accuracy of predictions.

Roadmap. In Sect. 2 we present some related work. In Sect. 3 we provide definitions and we describe the problem that we solve. In Sect. 4 we describe our datasets and the techniques that we use and in Sect. 5 we present our results. We conclude in Sect. 6.[2]

---

[1] Fabio Panetta, Chamber of Deputies, Rome, May 10, 2018.

[2] The views expressed in the article are those of the authors and do not involve the responsibility of the Bank of Italy.

2 Related Work

There has been an enormous amount of work on bankruptcy prediction. Here we present some of the most influential studies.

Initially, scholars focused on making a linear distinction among healthy companies and the ones that will eventually default. Among the most influencing pioneers in this field we can distinguish Altman [2] and Ohlson [20], both of whom made a traditional probabilistic econometric analysis. Altman, essentially defined a score, the Z discriminant score, which depends on several financial ratios (working capital/total assets, retained earnings/total assets, etc.) to asses the financial condition of a company. Ohlson on the other side, is using a linear regression (LR) logit model that estimates the probability of failure of a company. Some papers criticize these methods as unable to classify companies as viable or nonviable [6]. However, both approaches are used, in the majority of the literature, as a benchmark to evaluate more sophisticated methods.

Since these early works there has been a large number of works based on machine-learning techniques [16,18,21]. The most successful have been based on decision trees [12,15,17,24] and neural networks [4,7,11,19,23]. Typically, all these works use different datasets and different sets of features, depending on the dataset. Barboza et al. [5] compare such techniques with support vector machines and ensemble methods showing that ensemble methods and random forests perform the best.

These works mostly try to predict bankruptcy of a company. Our goal is to predict default (see Sect. 3). Furthermore, most of these papers use balance-sheet data (which are public).

Recently, Andini et al. [3] have used data from Italian Central Credit Register to assess the creditworthiness of companies in order to propose an improvement in the effectiveness of the assignment policies of the public guarantee programs.

Our dataset contains credit informations on the past behavior of loan repayment for each single firms of a very large set of companies. To our knowledge, this is the most extensive dataset used in the literature.

3 Firm-Default–Prediction Problem

There are many technical terms used to characterize debtors who are in financial problems: illiquidity, insolvency, default, bankruptcy, and so on. Most of the past research on prediction of failures addresses the concept of *firm bankruptcy*, which is the legal status of a company, in the public registers, that is unable to pay its debts. A firm is in *default* towards a bank, if it is unable to meet its legal obligations towards paying a loan. There are specific quantitative criteria that a bank may use to give a default status to a company.

3.1 Definition of *Adjusted Default Status*

The recent financial crisis has led to a revision and harmonization at international level of the concept of loan default. In general, default is the failure to pay interest or principal on a loan or security when due. In this paper we consider the classification of *adjusted default status*, which is a classification that the Italian National Central Bank (Bank of Italy) gives to a company that has a problematic debt situation towards the entire banking system. It represents a supervisory concept, whose aim is to extend the default credit status to all the loans of a borrower towards the entire financial system (banks, financial institutions, etc.). The term refers to the concept of the Basel II international accord of *default* of customers. According to this definition, a borrower is defined in default if its credit exposure has became significantly negative. In detail, to asses the status of adjusted default, Bank of Italy considers three types of negative exposures. They are the following, in decreasing order of severity: (1) A *bad (performing) loan* is the most negative classification; (2) an *unlikely to pay* (UTP) loan is a loan for which the bank has high probability to loose money; (3) A loan is *past due* if it is not returned after a significant period past the deadline.

Bank of Italy classifies a company in *adjusted default*, or *adjusted non performing loan* if it has a total amount of loans belonging to the aforementioned three categories exceeding certain pre-established proportionality thresholds [1]. Therefore, a firm's adjusted default classification derives from quantitative criteria and takes into account the company's debt exposure to the entire banking system.

If a company enters into an adjusted-default status then it is typically unable to obtain new loans. Furthermore, such companies are multiple times more likely to bankrupt in the future. For instance, out of the $13K$ companies that were classified in a status of adjusted default in December of 2015, 2160 (16.5%) were no longer active in 2016, having gone bankrupt or being in another similar bad condition. On the other hand, only 2.4% of the companies that were not in adjusted default status became bankrupt.

In this paper we attempt to predict whether a company will obtain an adjusted default status, although for brevity we may call it just default.

4   Data and Methods

In this section we describe the data on which we based our analysis and the machine-learning techniques that we used.

4.1   Dataset Description

Our analysis is based on two datasets. The first and most important in our work is composed of information on loans and the credit of a large sample of Italian companies. The second reports balance sheet data of a large sub-sample of medium-large Italian companies.

Credit data. The first dataset consists of a very large and high granular dataset of credit information about Italian companies belonging to the Italian central credit register (CCR). It is an information system on the debt of the customers of the banks and financial companies supervised by the Bank of Italy. Bank of Italy collects information on customers' borrowings from the intermediaries and notifies them of the risk position of each customer vis-à-vis the banking system. By means of the CCR the Bank of Italy provides intermediaries with a service intended to improve the quality of the lending of the credit system and ultimately to enhance its stability. The intermediaries report to the Bank of Italy on a monthly basis the total amount of credit due from their customers: data information about loans of 30, 000 euro or more and non-performing loans of any amount. The Italian CCR has three main goals: (1) to improve the process of assessing customer creditworthiness, (2) to raise the quality of credit granted by intermediaries, and to (3) strengthen the financial stability of the credit system.

The crucial feature of this database is the high granularity of credit information. It contains information for about $800K$ companies for each quarter of the the period of 2009–2014. The main features are shown in Table 1.

Table 1. Main attributes for the loan (L) and the balance-sheet (B) datasets.

ID	Description	ID	Description
L1	Granted amount of loans	B1	Revenues
L2	Used amount of loans	B2	ROE
L3	Bank's classification of firm	B3	ROA
L4	Average amount of loan used	B5	Total turnover
L5	Overdraft	B6	Total assets
L6	Margins	B7	Financial charges/operating margin
L7	Past due (loans not returned after the deadline)	B8	EBITDA
L8	Amount of problematic loans		
L9	Amount of non-performing loans		
L10	Amount of loans protected by a collateral		
L11	Value of the protection		
L12	Amount of forborne credit		

The Balance-sheets dataset. Our second dataset consists of the balance-sheet data of about $300K$ Italian firms. They are generally medium and large companies and they form a subset of the $800K$ companies with loan data. It contains balance-sheet information for each year from 2006 to 2014. The main features include those that regard the profitability of a company, such as return of equity (ROE) and return of assets (ROA); see Table 1 for a more extended list. Typically balance sheet data are public data and have been used extensively for bankruptcy prediction (e.g., see Barboza et al. [5] and references therein).

4.2 Machine-Learning Approaches

As we explain in Sect. 2, the first approaches for assessing the likelihood of companies to fail were based on some fixed scores; see the work by Altman [2]. Current approaches are based on more advanced machine-learning techniques. In this paper we follow the literature [5] by considering a set of diverse machine-learning approaches for predicting loan defaults.

In the first test we used five well-known machine-learning approaches. We provide a brief description of each of them, as provided by Wikipedia.

Decision Tree (DT): One of the most popular tool in decision analysis and also in Machine Learning. A decision tree is a flowchart-like structure in which each internal node represents a "test" on an attribute, each branch represents the outcome of the test, and each leaf node represents a class label (decision taken after computing all attributes). The paths from root to leaf represent classification rules.

Random Forest (RF): Random forest are an ensemble learning method for classification, regression and other tasks, that operate by constructing a multitude of decision trees at training time and outputting the class that is the mode of the classes. Random decision forests correct for decision trees' habit of overfitting to their training set.

Bagging (BAG): Bootstrap aggregating, also called bagging, is a machine learning ensemble meta-algorithm designed to improve the stability and accuracy of machine learning algorithms used in statistical classification and regression. It also reduces variance and helps to avoid overfitting. Although it is usually applied to decision tree methods, it can be used with any type of method. Bagging was proposed by Leo Breiman in 1994 to improve classification by combining classifications of randomly generated training sets.

AdaBoost (ADA): AdaBoost, short for Adaptive Boosting, is a machine learning meta-algorithm formulated by Yoav Freund and Robert Schapire, in 2003. It can be used in conjunction with many other types of learning algorithms to improve performance. The output of the other learning algorithms ('weak learners') is combined into a weighted sum that represents the final output of the boosted classifier. AdaBoost (with decision trees as the weak learners) is often referred to as the best out-of-the-box classifier.

Gradient boosting (GB): Gradient boosting is a machine learning technique for regression and classification problems, which produces a prediction model in the form of an ensemble of weak prediction models, typically decision trees. It builds the model in a stage-wise fashion like other boosting methods do, and it generalizes them by allowing optimization of an arbitrary differentiable loss function. That is, algorithms that optimize a cost function over function space by iteratively choosing a function (weak hypothesis) that points in the negative gradient direction.

Except for these standard techniques, we also combined the various classifiers in the following way. After learning two versions of each classifier, one with the default parameters of the `Python` `scikit` implementation and one with optimal parameters (to this end, we have used an exhaustive search over specified parameter values for each classifier, using the `sklearn.model. selection.GridSearchCV`), we execute all of them (10 in total) and if at least 3 classifiers predict that a firm will default then the classifier predicts default for that firm. The number 3 was chosen after experimentation. We call this ensemble approach **COMB**.

5   Experimental Results

The main goal of our study is to evaluate the extent to which we can predict whether a company will enter in a default state using data from past years. In particular, our goal is to predict whether a company that by December 2014 is not in default, will enter in default during one of the four trimesters of 2015. To do the prediction, we initially used data from the period of 2006–2014; however we noticed that using loan data running earlier than five trimesters before 2015 did not help. Therefore, for all the experimental results that we report here, we use the loan data from the last quarter of 2013 plus those from the four quarter of 2014 and the entire balance-sheet dataset from 2006 to 2014.

5.1   Evaluation Measures

We use a variety of evaluation measures to assess the effectiveness of our classifiers, which we briefly define. As usually, in a binary classification context, we use the standard concepts of true positive (TP), false positive (FP), true negative (TN), false negative (FN): For instance, FN is the number of firms that

	Predicted Default	Predicted Not Default
Default	**TP**	**FN**
Did not default	**FP**	**TN**

defaulted during 2015 but the classifier predicted that they will not default.

We now define the measures that we use:

- Precision: $\mathbf{Pr} = \dfrac{\mathbf{TP}}{\mathbf{TP} + \mathbf{FP}}$
- Recall: $\mathbf{Re} = \dfrac{\mathbf{TP}}{\mathbf{TP} + \mathbf{FN}}$
- F1-score: $\mathbf{F1} = 2 \cdot \dfrac{\mathbf{Pr} \cdot \mathbf{Re}}{\mathbf{Pr} + \mathbf{Re}}$
- Type-I Error: $\mathbf{Type\text{-}I} = \dfrac{\mathbf{FN}}{\mathbf{TP} + \mathbf{FN}}$
- Type-II Error: $\mathbf{Type\text{-}II} = \dfrac{\mathbf{FP}}{\mathbf{TN} + \mathbf{FP}}$
- Balanced Accuracy: $\mathbf{BACC} = 2 \cdot \frac{\mathbf{TP} \cdot \mathbf{TN}}{\mathbf{TP} + \mathbf{TN}}$

5.2   Datasets

In Sect. 4.1 we already described the datasets that we use. We perform two families of experiments. In the first one, we use only the loan data (as typically performed by Bank of Italy) to assess the probability of default. Then, we also combine this information with balance-sheet data. We have balance-sheet data available for 300K (out of 800K) companies. We decided to limit our study to these 300 K companies, as this allows us to compare the results in the case that we use only loan data and in the case that we use both loan and balanced-sheet data.

5.3   Balanced Versus Imbalanced Classes

The classification problem that we deal is very imbalanced: around 4.3% of the firms were in a default state in 2015. Therefore, as performed in prior work [5] we consider two cases. First we use the entire dataset, second we also create a balanced version by selecting all the firms that defaulted ($13.2K$) and an equal number of random firms that did not default, creating in this way a down-sampled balanced dataset of $26.4K$ firms.

5.4   Baselines

We evaluated the techniques presented in Sect. 4.2. To assess their effectiveness, we compare them with three basic approaches. The first one is a simple multino-mial Naïve Bayes (**MNB**) classifier. The second is a logistic regression (**LOG**) classifier. Finally, we created the following simple approach. We first measured the correlation of each feature with the target variables (refer to Table 1). We found the most significant ones (i.e., the ones that are mostly correlated with the target variable) are L3 (a bank's classification of the firm) and L7 (amount of loans not repaid after the deadline) for the loan dataset, and B2 (ROE) and B3 (ROA) for the balance sheet dataset. Then we built the simple classifier that outputs *default* if at least one of L3 or L7 are nonzero and *not default* otherwise for the loan dataset. We call this baseline **NAIVE**.

We gather the classification approaches that we use in Table 2.

Table 2. Baselines and classification algorithms.

ID method	Description
NAIVE	Naive classifier based on features correlation with target
MNB	Multinomial Bayesian classifier
LOG	Logistic Regression
GB	Gradient Boosting
RF	Random Forest
DT	Decision Tree
BAG	Bagging
ADA	AdaBoost
COMB	Combined method based on multiple classifiers

5.5   Prediction of Adjusted Default

We are now ready to predict whether companies will enter into an adjusted default state, as we explained in Sect. 3.1.

First we present the results for the original, imbalanced dataset. In Table 3 we present the results when we use only the loan dataset, whereas in Table 4 we present the results when we also use the balance-sheet data. The first finding is that the evaluation scores are rather low. This is in accordance to all prior work, indicating the difficulty of the problem. We observe that the machine-learning approaches perform better than the baselines, and the various algorithms trade off differently over the various evaluation measures. Random forests perform particularly well (in accordance with the findings of Barboza et al. [5]) and our combined approach (**COMB**) is able to trade off between precision and recall and give an overall good classification. Comparing Table 3 with Table 4 we see that the additional information provided by the balance-sheet data helps to improve the classification.

Table 3. Imbalanced training set; loan data. Higher values are better, except for Type-I and Type-II error.

	Pr	Re	F1	Type-I	Type-II	BACC
NAIVE	0.25	0.11	0.16	0.89	0.04	0.54
MNB	0.95	0.05	0.09	0.95	0.02	0.52
LOG	0.44	0.01	0.02	0.99	0.01	0.50
GB	0.63	0.22	0.33	0.78	0.01	0.61
RF	0.61	0.21	0.31	0.79	0.01	0.60
DT	0.27	0.29	0.28	0.71	0.03	0.63
BAG	0.53	0.19	0.28	0.81	0.01	0.59
ADA	0.56	0.20	0.30	0.80	0.01	0.60
COMB	0.52	0.32	0.40	0.68	0.01	0.66

In Tables 5 and 6 we present the results for the balanced dataset. There are some interesting findings here as well. First, as expected the classification accuracy improves (similarly to [5]). Second, we notice that the **NAIVE** classifier performs well (expected, as feature L3 takes into account several factors of the company's behavior); however the type-II error is high. Overall, **COMB** approach remains the best performer.

Table 4. Imbalanced training set; loan and balance-sheet data. Higher values are better, except for Type-I and Type-II error.

	Pr	Re	F1	Type-I	Type-II	BACC
NAIVE	0.29	0.14	0.20	0.89	0.06	0.55
MNB	0.95	0.06	0.09	0.95	0.03	0.52
LOG	0.46	0.02	0.03	0.99	0.02	0.50
GB	0.63	0.23	0.34	0.77	0.01	0.61
RF	0.68	0.25	0.37	0.75	0.01	0.62
DT	0.28	0.32	0.30	0.68	0.04	0.64
BAG	0.59	0.21	0.31	0.79	0.01	0.60
ADA	0.61	0.26	0.36	0.74	0.01	0.63
COMB	0.55	0.36	0.43	0.64	0.01	0.67

Table 5. Balanced training set; loan data. Higher values are better, except for Type-I and Type-II error.

	Pr	Re	F1	Type-I	Type-II	BACC
NAIVE	0.24	0.78	0.37	0.28	0.50	0.62
MNB	0.43	0.08	0.14	0.88	0.03	0.51
LOG	0.36	0.21	0.26	0.79	0.03	0.59
GB	0.23	0.67	0.34	0.33	0.10	0.78
RF	0.16	0.73	0.26	0.27	0.17	0.78
DT	0.10	0.69	0.17	0.31	0.30	0.69
BAG	0.16	0.69	0.25	0.31	0.17	0.76
ADA	0.24	0.65	0.35	0.35	0.09	0.78
COMB	0.20	0.69	0.31	0.31	0.13	0.78

Table 6. Balanced training set; loan and balance-sheet data. Higher values are better, except for Type-I and Type-II error.

	Pr	Re	F1	Type-I	Type-II	BACC
NAIVE	0.25	0.77	0.38	0.23	0.49	0.64
MNB	0.44	0.09	0.15	0.91	0.03	0.53
LOG	0.36	0.22	0.28	0.78	0.03	0.60
GB	0.19	0.78	0.30	0.22	0.15	0.81
RF	0.18	0.80	0.30	0.20	0.16	0.82
DT	0.10	0.71	0.18	0.29	0.26	0.72
BAG	0.17	0.75	0.27	0.25	0.17	0.79
ADA	0.18	0.76	0.29	0.24	0.16	0.80
COMB	0.19	0.84	0.31	0.16	0.16	0.84

5.6   A Practical Application: Probability of Default for Loan Subgroups

We now see an application of our classifier in an applied problem faced by Bank of Italy. We compare the best performing classifier (**COMB**) with a method commonly used to estimate the probability of one-year default by companies at aggregate level.

Consider a segmentation of all the companies (e.g., according to economic sector, geographical area, etc.). Often there is the need to estimate the *probability of default* (PD) of a loan in a given segment. A very simple approach, which is actually used in practice, is to simply take the ratio of the companies in the segment that went into default at year $T + 1$ over all the companies that were not in default in year T. We use this method as a baseline.

We now consider a second approach based on our classifier, which we call **COMB**. We estimate the PD by considering the amount of companies in the segment that are expected (using the **COMB** classifier) to go into default at year $T + 1$ compared to the total loans existing for the segment at the time T.

We use two different segmentations. A coarse one, in which the segments are defined by the economic sector (e.g. mineral extraction, manufacturing), and a finer one, which is defined by the combination of the economic sector and the geographic area, as defined by a value similar to the company's zip code.

In Table 7 we compare the two approaches for estimating the PD. As expected, in both segmentations the classifier-based approach is a winner, with the improvement being larger for the finer segmentation. In many cases the two approaches give the same result, typically because in these cases there are no companies that fail (PD equals 0).

Table 7. Comparison of the standard approach to estimate PD with the classifier-based one. "Mean error" is the average error between the predicted PD value and the real one. "Var error" is the variance of the error. "Superiority percentage" is the percentage of segments in which the predictor is better than the other; in the remaining ones we have the same performance.

Coarse segmentation	Baseline	COMB	Fine segmentation	Baseline	COMB
Mean error	0.11	0.048	Mean error	0.088	0.036
Var error	0.056	0.016	Var error	0.06	0.025
Superiority percentage	25.1%	45.6%	Superiority percentage	6.1%	19.5%

6   Conclusion

Business-failure prediction is a very important topic of study for economic analysis and the regular functioning of the financial system. Moreover the importance of this issue has greatly increased following the recent financial crisis. There have been many recent studies that have tried to predict the failure of companies using various machine-learning techniques.

In our study, we used for the first time credit information from the Italian Central Credit Register to predict the banking default of Italian companies, using Machine Learning techniques. We analyzed a very large dataset containing information about *almost all the loans of all the Italian companies*. Our first findings is that, as in the case of bankruptcy prediction, machine-learning approaches are able to outperform significantly simpler statistical approaches. Moreover, combining classifiers of different type can lead to even better results. Finally, using information on past loan data is crucial, but the additional use of balance-sheet data can improve classification even further.

We show that the combined use of loan data with balanced-sheet data leads to improved performance for predicting default. We conjecture that using loan data in the prediction of bankruptcy (where, typically, only balance-sheet data are being used) can improve further the performance.

Nevertheless, prediction remains an extremely hard problem. Yet, even slight improvement in the performance, can lead to savings of multiple hundreds of euros for the banking system. Thus our goal is to improve classification even further by combining our approaches with further techniques, such as neural-network based ones. Some preliminary results in which we use only neural networks are encouraging, even though are worse than the results we report here.

References

1. Methods and Sources: Methodological notes (2018). available on the website of the Banca d'Italia. https://www.bancaditalia.it/pubblicazioni/condizioni-rischiosita/en_STACORIS_note-met.pdf?language_id=1
2. Altman, E.: Predicting financial distress of companies: revisiting the z-score and zeta. In: Handbook of Research Methods and Applications in Empirical Finance, vol. 5 (2000)
3. Andini, M., Boldrini, M., Ciani, E., de Blasio, G., D'Ignazio, A., Paladini, A.: Machine learning in the service of policy targeting: the case of public credit guarantees, vol. 1206 (2019). https://www.bancaditalia.it/pubblicazioni/temi-discussione/2019/2019-1206/en_tema_1206.pdf
4. Atiya, A.: Bankruptcy prediction for credit risk using neural networks: a survey and new results. IEEE Trans. Neural Netw. **12**, 929–935 (2001). https://doi.org/10.1109/72.935101
5. Barboza, F., Kimura, H., Altman, E.: Machine learning models and bankruptcy prediction. Expert Syst. Appl. **83**(C), 405–417 (2017). https://doi.org/10.1016/j.eswa.2017.04.006
6. Begley, J., Ming, J., Watts, S.: Bankruptcy classification errors in the 1980s: an empirical analysis of Altman's and Ohlson's models. Rev. Acc. Stud. **1**, 267–284 (1996)
7. Boritz, J., Kennedy, D., Albuquerque, A.D.M.E.: Predicting corporate failure using a neural network approach. Intell. Syst. Account. Finance Manag. **4**(2), 95–111 (1995). https://doi.org/10.1002/j.1099-1174.1995.tb00083.x

8. Chen, M.Y.: Bankruptcy prediction in firms with statistical and intelligent techniques and a comparison of evolutionary computation approaches. Comput. Math. Appl. **62**(12), 4514–4524 (2011). https://doi.org/10.1016/j.camwa.2011.10.030

9. Cho, S., Hong, H., Ha, B.C.: A hybrid approach based on the combination of variable selection using decision trees and case-based reasoning using the Mahalanobis distance: For bankruptcy prediction. Expert Syst. Appl. **37**(4), 3482–3488 (2010). http://www.sciencedirect.com/science/article/pii/S0957417409009063

10. Erdogan, B.: Prediction of bankruptcy using support vector machines: an application to bank bankruptcy. J. Stat. Comput. Simul. - J STAT COMPUT SIM **83**, 1–13 (2012)

11. Fernández, E., Olmeda, I.: Bankruptcy prediction with artificial neural networks. In: Mira, J., Sandoval, F. (eds.) IWANN 1995. LNCS, vol. 930, pp. 1142–1146. Springer, Heidelberg (1995). https://doi.org/10.1007/3-540-59497-3_296

12. Gepp, A., Kumar, K.: Predicting financial distress: a comparison of survival analysis and decision tree techniques. Procedia Comput. Sci. **54**, 396–404 (2015)

13. Kumar, P.R., Ravi, V.: Bankruptcy prediction in banks and firms via statistical and intelligent techniques - a review. Eur. J. Oper. Res. **180**(1), 1–28 (2007). https://doi.org/10.1016/j.ejor.2006.08.043

14. Lee, S., Choi, W.S.: A multi-industry bankruptcy prediction model using backpropagation neural network and multivariate discriminant analysis. Expert Syst. Appl. **40**(8), 2941–2946 (2013). https://doi.org/10.1016/j.eswa.2012.12.009

15. Lee, W.C.: Genetic programming decision tree for bankruptcy prediction. In: 9th Joint International Conference on Information Sciences (JCIS 2006). Atlantis Press (2006)

16. Lin, W.Y., Hu, Y.H., Tsai, C.F.: Machine learning in financial crisis prediction: a survey. IEEE Trans. Syst. Man Cybern. - TSMC **42**, 421–436 (2012). https://doi.org/10.1109/TSMCC.2011.2170420

17. Martinelli, E., de Carvalho, A., Rezende, S., Matias, A.: Rules extractions from banks' bankrupt data using connectionist and symbolic learning algorithms. In: Proceedings of Computational Finance Conference (1999)

18. Nanni, L., Lumini, A.: An experimental comparison of ensemble of classifiers for bankruptcy prediction and credit scoring. Expert Syst. Appl. **36**(2), 3028–3033 (2009). https://doi.org/10.1016/j.eswa.2008.01.018

19. Odom, M., Sharda, R.: A neural network model for bankruptcy prediction. In: Proceedings of the 1990 IJCNN International Joint Conference on Neural Networks, vol. 2, pp. 163–168 (1990)

20. Ohlson, J.A.: Financial ratios and the probabilistic prediction of bankruptcy. J. Account. Res. **18**(1), 109–131 (1980)

21. Sarojini Devi, S., Radhika, Y.: A survey on machine learning and statistical techniques in bankruptcy prediction. Int. J. Mach. Learn. Comput. **8**, 133–139 (2018). https://doi.org/10.18178/ijmlc.2018.8.2.676

22. Wang, G., Ma, J., Yang, S.: An improved boosting based on feature selection for corporate bankruptcy prediction. Expert Syst. Appl. **41**(5), 2353–2361 (2014). http://www.sciencedirect.com/science/article/pii/S0957417413007872

23. Wang, N.: Bankruptcy prediction using machine learning. J. Math. Finance **07**, 908–918 (2017). https://doi.org/10.4236/jmf.2017.74049

24. Zhou, L., Wang, H.: Loan default prediction on large imbalanced data using random forests. TELKOMNIKA Indones. J. Electr. Eng. **10**, 1519–1525 (2012)

Convolutional Neural Networks, Image Recognition and Financial Time Series Forecasting

Argimiro Arratia[✉] and Eduardo Sepúlveda

Computer Science and Faculty of Mathematics and Statistics, Barcelona Tech (UPC), Barcelona, Spain
argimiro@cs.upc.edu, eduardo.sepulveda@estudiant.upc.edu

Abstract. Convolutional Neural Networks (CNN) are best known as good image classifiers. This model is recently been used for financial forecasting. The purpose of this work is to show that by converting financial information into images and feeding these financial-image representation to the CNN, it results in an improvement in classification.

Keywords: Convolutional Neural Networks · Recurrence plots · Time series · Forecasting

1 Introduction

Convolutional Neural Networks (CNN), whose first architecture harks back to the model proposed by LeCun et al. [5], has been empirically proven to do much better at classifying images (and general high dimension structures) than classical neural networks. A distinctive characteristic of CNN is that it exploits the local spatial coherence of images. By applying convolutions to small squares (or patches) of the input, through a sliding window that runs over the whole image, a CNN learns local features of the image and consequently preserves the spatial relationship between its pixels. Each convolution is determined by a *filter* (or *kernel*) which defines the size of the sliding window to capture the local information (feature extraction) of the image. Applying different filters (and convolutions) the CNN learns different feature maps, thus improving its ability to recognise specific patterns in the input data. For the mathematical details of the CNN model see [4].

In the realm of financial time series forecasting the motivation for using a CNN seems clearly its capability to take advantage of the (local) structural information within the data, ideally by learning feature maps (or their original filters) that represent specific patterns in the time series that is target for future values

A. Arratia—Supported by grant TIN2017-89244-R from MINECO (Ministerio de Economía, Industria y Competitividad) and the recognition 2017SGR-856 (MACDA) from AGAUR (Generalitat de Catalunya).

© Springer Nature Switzerland AG 2020
V. Bitetta et al. (Eds.): MIDAS 2019, LNAI 11985, pp. 60–69, 2020.
https://doi.org/10.1007/978-3-030-37720-5_5

prediction, such as those extracted from Technical Analysis; or patterns in time-dependent exogenous variables deemed as potential predictors, such as those obtained from Fundamental Analysis (see [1, Ch. 6] for a survey of Technical and Fundamental analysis in financial engineering).

However, the limited picture offered by the 1D nature of time series data could possibly restrict the recognition ability of a CNN. As it has been well studied in signal theory, some features of time series are best identified in the frequency domain rather than in the time domain; likewise, making a higher dimension representation of a time series may give a richer picture of its different features that a CNN can best recognise and take advantage.

In this paper we demonstrate the CNN improvement in financial time series prediction by preprocessing financial data as images before feeding them as inputs to the model. The transformation of numeric data to image is performed through *recurrence plots* (RP).

In the following section we explain the methodology of recurrence plot to transform numeric arrays into a matrix of bits (an image), we further explain details of the convolutional neural network model, and the data sets we use for our financial forecasting experiments. Then in Sect. 3 we report our experiments, which basically consists in comparing the performance in making predictions by a standard CNN versus a CNN endowed with a RP pre-processing unit of the input, and in two different scenarios: one on predicting direction of price of S&P 500 index, and the other on predicting financial distress of a collection of U.S. banks. In Sect. 4 we conclude.

2 Methods and Data

2.1 Recurrence Plots

Recurrence plots, introduced by Eckmann et al. [3], provides a visualization of the periodic nature of a trajectory through a phase space. Recurrence plots have been used in time series classification [6]. It is formalized as a matrix where each entry is given by the equation

$$R(i,j) = \Theta(\varepsilon - ||\boldsymbol{x}(i) - \boldsymbol{x}(j)||), \quad \boldsymbol{x}(\cdot) \in \mathbf{R}^m, i,j = 1\dots N \qquad (1)$$

where N is the number of states, $\boldsymbol{x}(i)$ is the subsequence observed at time i, $||\cdot||$ is a norm, ε is a threshold for closeness and Θ is the Heaviside function ($\Theta(z) = 0$, if $z < 0$, or 1 otherwise). Thus, if the m-dimensional trajectory of the time series at time i is close (with respect to some metric) to the subsequence observed at time j, there will be a 1 (or a yellow square, as in our image representation) at entry (i,j) of recurrence matrix; otherwise, the value is 0 (a dark purple square).

In our experiments we use the pairwise Euclidean distance for the RP norm $||\cdot||$. We observe that one can use RP beyond time series as a general pictorial representation of a similarity metric among multi-dimensional features of some other kind of numeric data apart from time series. We use it in that sense for the bankruptcy classification problem.

2.2 CNN Model

Convolutional Neural Networks (CNN) are made up of hidden nodes (or neurons), distributed through various layers, with learnable weights and biases. Each neuron receives several inputs and computes a weighted sum over them, and then passes the result through an activation function which gives an output. Popular choices for activation functions are: the logistic sigmoid ($\sigma(x) = 1/(1 + \exp(-x))$), the hyperbolic tangent ($\tanh(x) = 2/(1 + \exp(-2x)) - 1$), or the rectified linear units (ReLu, $R(x) = \max(0, x)$). The network's parameters are tuned by minimizing some loss function.

As opposed to regular neural networks, nodes in a CNN are not fully connected but only connected to a local region in the inputs. This local connectivity is attained by using convolutions instead of weighted sums. In each layer of the CNN, inputs are convolved with a weight array (referred as the filter or kernel) to create a feature map; that is, the weight array (kernel) which is of smaller dimension than the input, slides over the input and computes its dot product over each local region. The output of this feature map is then passed through a (non-linear) activation function (e.g. some of the three activation functions mentioned above), and the dimension of this transformed feature map is subsequently reduced by *spatial pooling* (or subsampling). For example, by considering Max, Average or Sum of values. In practice, Max Pooling has been shown to work best. The objective of pooling is to down-sample an input representation, reducing its dimension and allowing for assumptions to be made about features contained in the sub-regions binned.

The procedure is repeated layer by layer (the number of layer determines the *depth* of the network); that is, in each subsequent layer $l = 2, \ldots, D$, the input feature map obtained from previous layer $l - 1$, by convolutions and transformation through activation function and pooled, is convolved with a set of M_l kernels to create a new feature map corresponding to the current layer l.

The dimension of the convolution operator accommodates to the dimension of the data. For one-dimensional input, as is the case of time series, $x = \{x(t) : t = 1, \ldots, N\}$, one-dimensional (1D) convolutions with kernels w_h, for $h = 1, \ldots, M$ with $M < N$, can be used, which are formally defined as

$$s(t, h) = (w_h \star x)(t) = \sum_{n=-\infty}^{\infty} x(n)w_h(t - n) \tag{2}$$

For two-dimensional input, as is the case of images, $(I(i, j))_{1 \leq i, j \leq N}$, the appropriate convolutions must be two-dimensional (2D) on kernel matrices $(K_h(i, j))_{1 \leq i, j \leq M}$:

$$s(i, j, h) = (K_h \star I)(i, j) = \sum_m \sum_n I(i - m, j - n)K_h(m, n) \tag{3}$$

We use Keras, the Python Deep Learning library[1], for CNN computations. We adopt the nomenclature of Keras, where a 1D CNN is denoted Conv1D, and a 2D CNN is Conv2D.

2.3   Datasets

S&P 500 Index. For our stock market prediction experiment the dependent variable or target for prediction is the sign of the Standard & Poor's 500 equity premium (GSPCep). This is the difference of logarithms of the price returns, including dividends, and the risk-free interest rate:

$$GSPCep(t) = \log\left(\frac{P(t) + D12(t)}{P(t-1)}\right) - \log(r(t) + 1)$$

where $P(t)$ and $D12(t)$ are, respectively, the price and the 12-month moving sums of dividends paid on the S&P 500 index at time t, and $r(t)$ is the interest rate of the three months U.S. Treasury bill. Our target of prediction is essentially the direction of price with reference to the risk-free interest rate. We consider as exploratory variables or features the past history of the equity premium, up to three lags, and past history of its variance estimated as the square of GSPCep, up to two lags.

This financial data has been retrieved from Amit Goyal's webpage, which builds upon a data collected by Robert Schiller for his statistical analysis of S&P 500. The data is sampled on a monthly basis and ranges from 1990 to 2015.

Bank Data. The data consist of arrays with 106 exploratory variables pertaining to financial indicators drawn from quarterly financial reports of U.S. banks, plus 1 response variable which is categorical taking value 1 to indicate a bankrupt entity, or 0 otherwise. There are 5152 of these arrays, each representing the financial situation of a bank. Each bank has at least 8 quarter periods of financial data reporting. This financial information have been retrieved from the Federal Deposit Insurance Corporation (FDIC), who maintains a list of U.S. insured banks that went bankrupt during the period 1992–2017.

3   Experiments and Results

The experiments consist in comparing the Convolutional Neural Network's performance with two different processing of its data inputs. The first one consists on feeding the one-dimensional numerical data directly as input to our CNN. The second one consists on first pre-processing the numerical data into images using the Recurrence Plot technique. Each image represents a time series which is categorized according to its response variable. These images provide the input for our CNN.

---

[1] https://keras.io/.

We will compare the performance of the models with respect to accuracy in classification, loss in training, AUC, Matthews Correlation and 10-fold cross-validation. The use of cross-validation in time series data is justified in [2].

We perform the experiments in two different financial scenarios: (1) to predict direction of price of the S&P 500 index; (2) to predict the possibility of bankruptcy in a set of U.S. banks.

3.1 CNN Specifications

We build two types of Convolutional Neural Network models using the Keras library in Python. In both cases we used sequential modeling because is the easiest way to build a model layer by layer in Keras. Since our goal is to test the possible enhancement in classification of a CNN with a RP we will not care about tuning in any sophisticated way the inner workings of the CNN and rather work with a basic structure upon which we feed the input processed as image through the recurrence plot method, or not. In the following list we detail the structure of the Convolutional Neural Network in our models and difference between them. The main difference is the pre-processing of data inputs.

Conv1D: Consists of one convolutional layer made of one-dimensional convolutions with kernels of size 2 and 64 nodes. Inputs are numeric arrays. The activation function we use is the ReLU, which works quite well in practice and is less computationally expensive than tanh and sigmoid because it involves simpler mathematical operations. The Pooling layer will be produced with Max pooling.

Conv2D + RP: For this model the inputs (arrays of numbers) are first pre-processed with the recurrence plot (RP) method to produce corresponding images (matrices of 0 and 1). Then follows a convolutional layer made of two-dimensional convolutions with kernels of size 2×2 and 64 nodes, a ReLu activation function, and a Max pooling layer.

Compiling the Model. Compiling the model takes three parameters: optimizer, loss and metrics.

1. The optimizer controls the learning rate. We will be using "Adam" as our optimizer because it is generally a good optimizer to use for many cases. The Adam optimizer adjusts the learning rate throughout training. The learning rate determines how fast the optimal weights for the model are calculated. A smaller learning rate may lead to more accurate weights (up to a certain point), but the time it takes to compute the weights will be longer.
2. We used *binary crossentropy* for our loss function. This is the most common choice for classification problem with two labels.
3. Metrics: we use the accuracy metric to see the accuracy score on the validation set when we train the model.

Train the Model. We will use the "fit()" function with the following parameters: training data (train X), target data (train Y), validation data, epochs number and batch number.

The number of epochs is how many times the entire dataset is passed forward and backward through the neural network. The more epochs we run, the more the model will improve, up to a certain point. After that point, the model will stop improving during each epoch. The batch size is the total number of training examples present in a single batch. For example we can divide the dataset of 60 examples into batches of 12 then it will take 5 iterations to complete 1 epoch. In our experiments we set epoch to 10, and batch to 1.

Validation Data. We will use the test set provided to us in our dataset, which we have split into X test and Y test.

3.2 Experiment 1: Predicting Direction of SP500

Data Preparation. As detailed in Sect. 2.3, the data consists of arrays of 5 exploratory variables (lags 1, 2, and 3 of the GSPCep series and lags 1 and 2 of the square of the series, sampled monthly), plus 1 response variable which is categorical taking value 1 to indicate an increase of the (monthly) price of S&P500, or 0 otherwise. There are 300 of these arrays, representing the multivariate series ranging from 1990 to 2015. We apply a rolling window of size 12 (12 months of data or arrays) to predict next month price direction, and make forward steps of 1 month. Hence, each RP uses 12 periods of financial data.

In the first model (Conv1D) we use as "training X" an input array with the numerical values of the variables of the 12 periods of time and as "training Y" we will use a categorical input array of 0 and 1 for each time series.

On the other hand, for model Conv2D+RP we convert this training (X, Y) numerical input array to image using recurrence plots. In this way we obtain images (a matrix input) which are then fed to the 2D-Convolutional Neural Network.

We can observe in Fig. 1 that the images created by recurrence plot present differences when comparing them between their categories (Down = 0 and Up = 1).

Results. We repeat each experiment 100 times and obtain the following average results for each CNN model reported in Table 1.

Table 1. Performance of CNN without/with RP for S&P500 price prediction

	Acc	Loss	10-fold CV	AUC	Matthews cor.
Conv1D	0.52	5.75	61.1% (±4.16%)	0.65	−0.102
Conv2D + RP	0.63	2.69	63.22% (±0.93%)	0.66	−0.0026

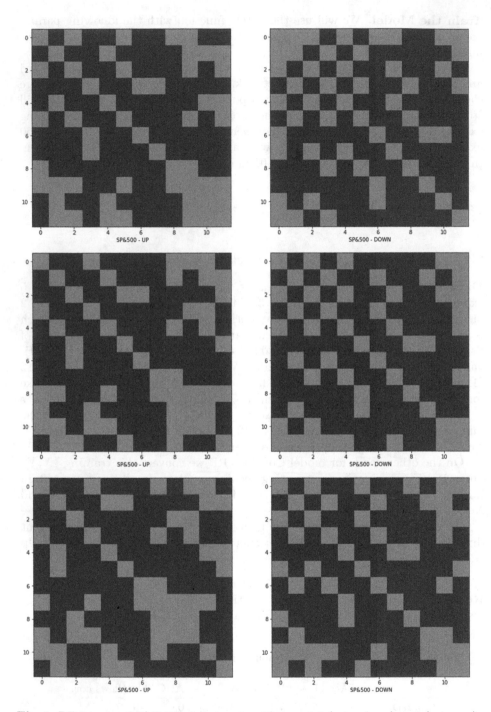

Fig. 1. RP images of S&P 500 data inputs with target 0 (price down) or 1 (price up)

We observed that by making a previous processing of the data by recurrence plot transforming our numerical data to images, we obtain better results consistently improving the accuracy, the AUC, Matthews correlation, while reducing the loss, and the 10-fold CV shows that the combined model Conv2D+RP generalizes well.

3.3 Experiment 2: Bankruptcy Detection

Data Preparation. We select the data of eight periods of time (quarters) for each bank and scale the data column by column by min - max method. We added the response variable classifying if the bank will fail or not in the next period of time.

For the first model (Conv1D) we used the input data as stated above for our CNN. But for the second model (Conv2D+RP) we convert the numeric time series data to images (recurrence plot) and give the image as input to our CNN.

In Fig. 2 we observe the recurrence plot of three pairs of banks classified as non - bankrupt and another as bankrupt. We can see a clear difference between the graphics which indicates an adequate classification already given by the RP method alone.

Results. Using CNN's with a similar configuration in both cases, and reproducing each experiment 100 times, we obtain the (average) results reported in Table 2.

Table 2. Performance of CNN without/with RP for Bankruptcy Detection

	Acc	Loss	10-fold CV	AUC	Matthews cor.
Conv1D	0.82	3.27	58.91% (±17.98%)	0.72	0.42
Conv2D + RP	0.94	1.01	93.75% (±0.07%)	0.83	0.67

The improvement in accuracy, AUC, Matthews correlation and decrease in loss are significant when pre-processing data with RP before feeding it to the 2D Convolutional Neural Network.

4 Conclusions

We have shown that by making a previous processing of the input by recurrence plot transformation of our numerical data to images, we obtain better classification results as measured by five different metrics of classification performance.

We have used a standard norm (Euclidean norm) for the definition of recurrence plots. Other norms are possible, in particular ones more suitable for capturing similarities among financial time series, like, for example, a correlation based metric. It would be interesting to see the difference in performance of Conv2D+RP model under different norms underlying the definition of the RP method.

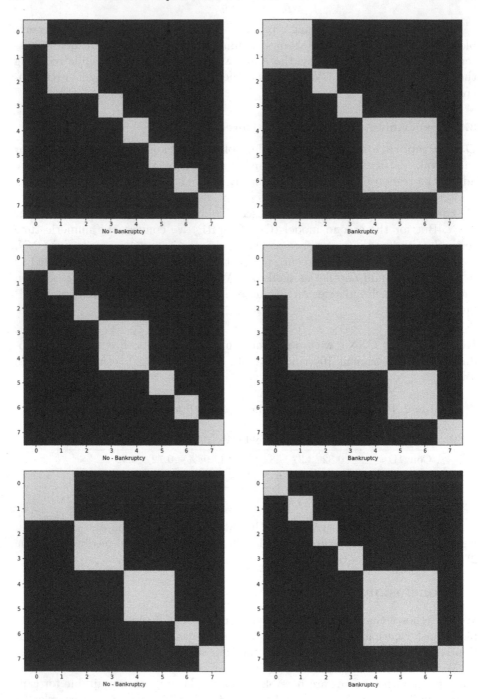

Fig. 2. RP images of U.S. bank data with target 1 (bankrupt) or 0 (non-bankrupt)

References

1. Arratia, A.: Computational Finance: An Introductory Course with R. Atlantis Press (2014)
2. Bergmeir, C., Hyndman, R.J., Koo, B.: A note on the validity of cross-validation for evaluating autoregressive time series prediction. Comput. Stat. Data Anal. **120**, 70–83 (2018)
3. Eckmann, J.P., Kamphorst, S.O., Ruelle, D.: Recurrence plots of dynamical systems. Europhys. Lett. **5**(9), 973–977 (1987)
4. Goodfellow, I., Bengio, Y., Courville, A.: Deep Learning. The MIT Press, Cambridge (2016)
5. LeCun, Y., Bottou, L., Bengio, Y., Haffber, P.: Gradient-based learning applied to document recognition. Proc. IEEE **86**, 2278–2324 (1998)
6. Silva, D.F., De Souza, V.M., Batista, G.E.: Time series classification using compression distance of recurrence plots. In: 2013 IEEE 13th International Conference on Data Mining, pp. 687–696. IEEE (2013)

Mining Business Relationships
from Stocks and News

Thomas Kellermeier[1], Tim Repke[1(✉)], and Ralf Krestel[1,2]

[1] Hasso Plattner Institute, University of Potsdam, Potsdam, Germany
thomas.kellermeier@student.hpi.de, tim.repke@hpi.de
[2] University of Passau, Passau, Germany
ralf.krestel@uni-passau.de

Abstract. In today's modern society and global economy, decision making processes are increasingly supported by data. Especially in financial businesses it is essential to know about how the players in our global or national market are connected. In this work we compare different approaches for creating company relationship graphs. In our evaluation we see similarities in relationships extracted from *Bloomberg* and *Reuters* business news and correlations in historic stock market data.

Keywords: Market analysis · Text mining · Entity relationships

1   Introduction

Financial markets play a fundamental role in today's global market economy. The strategic decision making process nowadays is supported by large-scale data analysis and by monitoring stock markets, decision makers can learn a lot. By buying and selling stocks, investors influence their value, e.g. by offering more when demand is high, they drive the price per share up. Following the Efficient Market Hypothesis [2,9], the investments can be interpreted as trust in positive future performance and in sum as an approximation of a company's intrinsic value. In the past, large efforts have been undertaken to understand and partially foresee the temporal evolution of stock markets and thereby reduce the risk of such investments for investors.

In this paper, we aim to identify relationships between publicly traded companies based on similar behaviour of their stock price movements and their mentions in business news.

Knowing about these inherent links may guide and support further analyses. For example, when assessing the credit risk of a new corporate client, the risk officer compares a number of factors to similar prior cases. To this end, we propose methods to construct weighted similarity graphs based on stocks and news texts that can be used to measure the similarity of companies.

Thoughtful preprocessing and feature selection is an important task for NLP [6]. By having methods to test or support NLP tasks with relationship information from stock markets, more sophisticated models can be developed. Some

V. Bitetta et al. (Eds.): MIDAS 2019, LNAI 11985, pp. 70–84, 2020.
https://doi.org/10.1007/978-3-030-37720-5_6

potential applications for improving text-based features in this context: Concept maps [22]; bag-of-keywords [27]; sentiment WordNet [17,34]. Incorporating relational features into artificial neural networks, most notably node embeddings or a graph convolutional layers has been shown to improve models in many areas of application [5].

Another use case for using business relationships and stock relationships is the observation and analysis of financial markets. In order to measure the value and credit risk of a company, competitors, suppliers, subsidiaries and other related companies might be considered to give a better assessment. Both business and stock relationships can be incorporated into a corporate graph and therefore support in understanding the complex net of relationships among companies.

In this work we provide an overview of approaches to generate weighted company relationship graphs from both text and stock data. Our comparison of these features yields important information about applicability of these approaches in different contexts.

2 Related Work

There are numerous approaches to model economic variables, for example utilizing econometrics, Natural Language Processing (NLP) and machine learning. Predicting a stock's future behaviour is among the main research topics. Although the stock market's future is unforeseeable, this problem receives great attention. It is a controversial topic and lacks a good theoretical foundation to justify forecasts on finance markets. As a naive example, one could take a model that always predicts rising stock prices – given enough time, this model will show great precision/recall scores thanks to global economic growth, which is only interrupted by crises where not even experts manage to project reliable time frames. By ignoring these issues and applying machine learning approaches in sandbox like environments, studies often do not fully reflect the problem space and therefore erroneously promise positive results. The related work presented in this section includes stock prediction, however we focus on their underlying methods and data to model financial markets.

With the high interest in prediction models a vast amount of data is available to researchers. Some studies focus on predicting the trend of stock prices via technical indicators like Bollinger Bands, momentum or Moving Average Convergence Divergence (MACD) [1,21,23]. Others consider the whole market instead of separate stocks by predicting a stock index or volatility index [6]. In this work we propose an approach to identify linked stock behaviour, so we focus on separate stocks instead of technical indicators or market indices. Although the studies above target other objectives, they need to tackle similar problems of data preparation to normalise the noisy and stochastic nature of stock markets.

Correlating stock prices requires intensive regression analysis, which is related to predictability of time series in the context of econometrics and statistics. Methods like cross-correlation, mutual information and Granger Causality are proposed to measure and compare financial time series. Often enough, machine learning models are applied without dealing with systematic errors in the raw economic data in the assumption that those models will learn to ignore problematic issues like noise on their own. Studies with more economical or statistical background investigate the characteristics and quality of economic variables.

The selection of the dataset itself plays a crucial role in the feasibility of a classification or regression problem. Sun et al. [30] report 70 % accuracy for their matrix factorization model during training but only 51 % on test data which is not a significant improvement compared to random guessing. Lee et al. [21] present a Random Forest Classifier for predicting separate stock prices with an accuracy 22.2 % higher than random guessing. Although results like these sound promising, it could be the consequence of an unsafe evaluation. Among various factors influencing an experiments outcome, models without cross-validation are prone to the "lucky sample effect", as demonstrated by Hsu et al. [16]. The time series might be lacking ergodic properties and therefore report erroneously high accuracy.

Kim et al. [19] apply a rule-based classifier on stocks from the energy sector of the US stock market. They calculate the cross-correlation among pairs of stocks and predict trends by considering the lagged stock price of another highly cross-correlated stock. Even though they select only highly cross-correlating pairs, potential spurious correlation are not considered which might arise due to unfiltered autocorrelations. As already pointed out by Granger et al. [13], misspecification like omitted variables or autocorrelations can lead to spurious regression. Ruiz et al. [29] exploit these auto-dependencies of stock prices by training Auto Regression and Vector Auto Regression models with the Ordinary Least Squares (OLS) method to predict the daily closing price. Their approach combines stock price data with numerical features extracted from Twitter, e.g. number of retweets. They do not inspect their data for homoscedasticity, which is one of the requirements of the Gauss-Markov theorem for OLS [14].

Instead of proving the predictability of a new introduced features by feeding it into a prediction model, Vlastakis et al. [31] apply a regression analysis between the demand for market-related information and market variables like volatility and stock prices. The overall information demand is represented by Google's Search Volume Index for the search keyword S&P 500 and they conclude, that some relationships exist with a high certainty.

Kosapattarapim et al. [20] presents a very detailed procedure on inspecting Granger Causality between the stock exchange index of Thailand and the exchange rate between Thai Baht against US dollars. To ensure that the preconditions hold, they inspect unit roots and co-integration relationships. Their results indicate an unidirectional causality from stock prices to exchange rate.

For a more conscious inspection of non-linear auto-dependencies in finance time series, Dionisio et al. [7] compare the normalised mutual information with Pearson's r for several stock price indices. Referring to related work, they recall the assumption of a strong relationship between entropy, dependence and predictability. To exclude the linear auto-dependencies, they filter the data by taking the residuals of an autoregressive–moving-average process. Unlike the linear correlation, mutual information still indicates a significant dependency on the residuals without any foreknowledge on the theoretical probability distribution or the type of dependency.

Since external information related to stock markets is not directly observable, meaningful proxies are extracted from unstructured data like forum posts, news, social media and SEC filings. The most popular text sources are financial news [17,27,34] because they are expected to represent new events influencing the financial market. Their importance is mostly reflected within the stock prices of the directly following days and loses its meaning over a longer time period [6]. Therefore, many scientists incorporate news for short-time prediction models [18]. They consider the news and the previous daily stock prices to predict the intraday price movement for the next day. Various methods for extracting abstract representations of news have been proposed over the last years.

Ding et al. [6] compare linear and non-linear approaches for prediction using events-based document representations without incorporating historical stock price data. They extract events by applying Open Information Extraction (OIE) on news articles from *Reuters* and *Bloomberg*. Thereby, each article is transformed into a tuple of subject, predicate verb and object.

Previous work usually only considers one company for predicting its future stock price as pointed out by Akita et al. [1]. They instead feed related articles and historical prices of ten companies within the same industry at once into a LSTM to predict the close prices of all ten companies by regression analysis. *Nikkei newspapers* are preprocessed using Paragraph Vectors which learns fixed-length feature vectors from variable-length texts. Their market simulation indicates that incorporating multiple companies from the same industry is very effective for stock price prediction.

A recent approach by Chen et al. [5] explores the setup and application of a corporate graph for a prediction model. A graph is proposed which contains nodes representing stock companies from Shanghai Stock Exchange and Shenzhen Stock Exchange and their shareholders. The weighted edges between those nodes indicate the shareholding ratio. They conclude that such relational data can improve the performance of stock prediction.

3 Relationships from News

In this work we propose to construct two company relationship graphs, one based on stock price movements, and the other on financial news. The literature on stock prediction has shown, that news articles impact financial markets [18] and can be used as a proxy for business relationship. If an announcement was made or any relevant information like a SEC filing was released by a company, financial news report it as fast as possible. Longer reports put it even into a bigger picture, provide some background information and refer to possible competitors. In this section we describe how we construct a relationship graph from a collection of news articles. Therefore, we introduce an effective baseline to extract company names and match them to their respective stock symbol. Furthermore we discuss different approaches to assign weights to relationship edges in the graph.

Data. We use the financial news dataset[1] released by Ding et al. [6]. It contains news articles from Reuters[2] (106,519 documents) and Bloomberg[3] (448,395 documents) covering the time period from 2006-10-20 to 2013-11-26. We discard duplicate articles as well as articles with less than 300 characters.

After filtering, there are 542,517 articles left. While Reuters articles are equally distributed over all covered years, most of the Bloomberg articles in our dataset were published after 2010.

Building a Relationship Graph. We assume that companies related in any context will be mentioned together in at least a few articles. In the following, the simultaneous mentioning of two companies within one article is called co-occurrence.

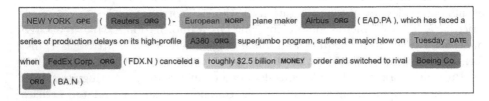

Fig. 1. Reuters article *"FedEx cancels Airbus A380 order, switches to Boeing"*, published on 2006-11-07, with recognised named entities.

Named Entity Recognition. First of all, we have to identify occurrences of every mentioned company. We observe a high recall of identified organisations. Although some entities might be falsely identified as an organisation, we see that later processing steps usually filter them out. We use SpaCy[4] to extract entities and only keep those that are classified as an organisation, which in the definition of SpaCy could be any company, agency or institution. Of the originally 40.7 million entities recognised in the over 500k articles, we keep 9.6 million organisation entities for further processing. Note, that these company mentions have numerous aliases and are not written consistently. For example, some authors might use a product of the company (e.g. *Google* instead of *Alphabet*) or just a representative such as the CEO (e.g. *Steve Jobs* instead of *Apple*). With the help of an aspect based product-centric model [24], we tested the performance of our graph construction model using proxies like products or representatives. We found 19k occurrences of people as representatives of companies. When using those in our evaluation, we saw now no overall improvement. Thus, only direct mentions without proxies are considered in the remainder of this work.

---

[1] https://drive.google.com/drive/folders/0B3C8GEFwm08QY3AySmE2Z1daaUE.
[2] https://www.reuters.com.
[3] https://www.bloomberg.com.
[4] https://spacy.io.

Named Entity Linking. Out of all organisation entities, only those are of interest which can be linked to a company from the S&P 500 market index. The official company name is provided by the stock dataset and linked to the correct stock prices by its stock symbol. The names contain suffixes like *Inc.* or *Limited* which are usually left out in the news. To establish the link between occurrences in news and the full corporate name, we use regular expressions to normalise names and remove extensions.

If the regular expression reduced both strings to their least common sequence and they are completely equal, the extracted entity is assumed to match the examined stock company. In the end, 436k related company names were extracted which are distributed over 127k articles. Because occurrences were only found for 443 companies, the remaining companies are removed.

Sometimes, Bloomberg articles already include stock symbols in parentheses following the company mentions, as can be seen from Fig. 1. Because this is the case for roughly 10% of the cases, we can not solely rely on this information for linking entities. Instead, we use it for evaluating our approach since the information was added by the author and therefore is assumed to be accurate. Each stock symbol in parenthesis is compared to the stock symbol of our linked entity, resulting in over 99.8% matches for the previously extracted 436k occurrences.

In the example in Fig. 1, two of the four organisations are linked to stock prices, whereas the remaining two are not considered since they are not components of the market index and thereby not contained by the data covered in this work.

Weighting Co-occurrence Edges. As mentioned before, we consider the co-occurrence of company mentions in the same article as a relationship. For more fine-grained interpretation of the resulting relationship graph, we add weights to the edges for which we propose three different metrics. First, we consider *Number of Articles* a co-occurrence appears in. This feature does not account for the number or distance of occurrences for two companies within one article. It rather measures the co-occurrences across the whole text corpus instead of weighting the connection within one article. The *Minimum Distance* takes the intra-article connection into account by calculating the distance for each possible pair of company names within one article. The shortest distance is kept for this article and averaged across all other distances in the corpus. This metric is based on the assumption that direct comparisons are drawn for strongly connected companies, which should be reflected by smaller distances on average. Lastly, the *Pairwise Distance* is a more sophisticated approach. It accounts for the multiple inter- and intra-article co-occurrences for which we use a scan line algorithm to traverse all mentions of these two companies in an article and pair these up while avoiding a too high distance. Similar to the previous approach, all distances are averaged but, in addition, each pair is considered instead of only considering the best one for each article.

We evaluate the different weighting approaches later by comparing the resulting graphs to the relationships we find in stock data.

4 Relationships from Stocks

The second company relationship graph we use in our work is based on stock price movements. The naive approach to define relationships is the correlation between the time series of indicators such as daily open and close values of two stocks. However, the general performance of a marketplace influences the individually traded stocks and therefore simple approaches will find strong pairwise correlation between all stocks. Therefore, we have to ensure that the time series are independent of exogenous variables and free of autocorrelation and heteroscedasticity to the greatest possible extent. Such malicious properties distort statistical inference resulting in meaningless findings. In econometrics, statistical methods are applied to financial time series to deal with spurious correlations [33] and conclude with meaningful cross-correlation coefficients. In the following, we refer to cross-correlation when talking about correlation. In this section we will describe the data, methods to normalise the time series for removing external influences, and how we construct a weighted relationship graph from historic stock market data.

Data. In this work we use historic stock market data collected between 2010 and 2016 for stocks listed in the S&P 500 index[5]. Each stock's daily open, high, low, close and volume values (OHLCV) is given in US dollar, all values are already accounted for stock splits and adjusted to the last price. Thus, price values of affected stocks in 2010 are rectified to have the same meaning as in 2016. For linking stock prices with occurrences in the previously introduced news dataset, we will be using the company names in the securities table from the same published dataset. We discard data after 2013-11-29, so that relationships we extract are based on data from the same time period as our news corpus. However, the financial news before 2010 will be used, even though no stock prices are collected for this time period, since relational features are assumed to have a long-term impact, so incorporating information from news between 2006 and 2010 is helpful. To account for acquisitions, mergers, dual-class listings, or bankruptcies of components in the index, we only consider stocks that are part of the index by the end of 2016. In addition to the stock prices, overall measurements of the performance and the confidence at the NYSE for the same period as the stock prices need to be considered. Therefore, we use the CBOE Volatility Index (VIX)[6] and the S&P 500 index (GSPC)[7]. There appears to be a strong negative relationship between volatility and stock market returns [10]. Most notable bursts of the VIX happened in 2010 and 2011 and are hypothesized to be caused by important steps during the European debt crisis[8]. Another burst is assumed to be a consequence of the *1000-point plunge* of the DOW Jones index

---

[5] https://www.kaggle.com/dgawlik/nyse, https://nemozny.github.io/datasets/.
[6] https://www.kaggle.com/lp187q/vix-index-until-jan-202018.
[7] https://www.kaggle.com/benjibb/sp500-since-1950.
[8] https://money.cnn.com/2011/08/08/markets/vix_fear_index/index.htm.

on the 24th of August in 2015, which in turn was a consequence of a rout in the Chinese market pulling down stock markets all over the world[9].

The preselection ensures the complete stock prices of 467 companies for all 985 trading days from 2010-01-04 to 2013-11-29.

Normalising Stock Movements. The previously described data has to be transformed to fulfil preconditions for the correlation analysis, namely the time series consist of independently and identically distributed samples [11]. Therefore, we combine different methods to remove shared external influences and existing autocorrelation, ensure homoscedasticity and apply autoregressive models to remove any remaining irrelevant patterns.

Stationarity. An assumption of the methods we employ to detect relationships between the financial time series is, that the data is stationary. Stock prices however follow the ever growing market and are thus non-stationary and are assumed to contain a unit root [28]. The unit root, namely the influence of the market, prevents the series to return to stationary mean and can be accounted for by differencing the time series taking the absolute or relative differences between each sample [8]. In the following we will use relative differences to account for different levels of stocks. Hong et al. [15] provide empirical findings about recurring patterns in returns including that open-to-open returns are more volatile than close-to-close returns, while Wang et al. [32] provide evidence that intra-day (open-to-close) and overnight (close-to-open) returns have significantly different properties concluding that one shall not mix them. Lastly, Li et al. [23] consider daily open-to-close prices arguing that it is less prone to seasonality and the more volatile non-trading gaps across weekends and holidays. Results for our data coincide with related work and show a moderate negative skew (-0.1 in average) for open-to-open/close-to-close returns and a slightly positive skew (0.06 in average) for the distribution of intra-day returns. Because of their more normal like distributions, relative intra-day returns are used for the remainder of this work.

Homoscedasticity. An important assumption for correlation is, that the data is homoscedastic, that is homogeneity of volatility in the context of time series. Stock prices, however, are heteroscedastic [26], most likely because exogenous factors are left out. Some statistical methods can be employed to normalise the data, for example with the GARCH model [25] or other robust regression methods such as weighted least squares regression. In this work, we use the Box-Cox transformation [3] for heuristic data stabilization by a simple power transformation. The model's power parameter is determined by maximising the log-likelihood function on the previously modified relative intra-day return. Since this general transformation is not a panacea to the problem, we also apply individually fitted autoregressive models on top of that.

---

[9] https://money.cnn.com/2015/08/24/investing/stocks-markets-selloff-china-crash-dow/index.html.

Exogenous Variables. Financial markets are prone to a number of external influences which are usually not accounted for by the previously described regression models on stock prices. If the economy is doing well or experiences a period of uncertainty, this will be likely reflected in all stock prices. Hence, omitting exogenous variable is another reason for spurious correlations [12]. A greater correlation between stock prices can be caused by a shared external factor which is the common market performance in this case. To have a better representation for the intrinsic performance of a single stock, its returns need to be normalised regarding the shared performance of the market. Further, the underlying movement of a stock price might even more be biased by the sentiment of the according industry section. Stocks from the same industry will therefore have a high cross-correlation without revealing specific relationships. We counteract exogenous influences by subtracting the average return value of a stock's industry sector. Alternatively, we can normalise by the S&P 500 market index instead of the separate industry averages. The impact of this alternate normalisation step will be examined later when setting up the graph based on the extracted cross-correlations.

Autoregression. Even after all previous normalisation steps, some autoregressive patterns may remain. Autoregressive models describe time series by a function of their past values along with an error term, known as the residual. The residuals are assumed to be free from linear autocorrelation [7] and therefore, if applicable, can be used to identify relationships between stocks. We use an autoregressive moving average model (ARMA) [29], that assumes lagged values and error terms for the same stationary and univariate time series. The model hyper-parameters are determined with the Box-Jenkins method [4]. We applied the ARMA model to 82 stocks for which autocorrelation was observable with this method. Even if the model wasn't applied to a time series, we refer to the unchanged data as the residuals in the following. On top, we apply a Generalised Autoregressive Conditional Heteroscedasticity Model (GARCH) on the residuals of the ARMA mean process to remove any remaining unstable volatility in the normalised stock prices. Because the actual volatility can not be observed directly and the data is ensured to be stationary, we use the squared residuals as a proxy. As the last step of our data normalisation we divide the ARMA residuals by the conditional volatility calculated with the GARCH model. For the 161 stocks where the GARCH model isn't applicable, we divide the residuals by the overall standard deviation to keep the resulting time series at the same scale.

Building a Relationship Graph. The data normalisation process is very involved to remove any influences on a stock price development that are not inherent to its intrinsic value. Obviously, some autocorrelation is still contained in the data since all economic decision making is somewhat linked. We conducted a series of tests to ensure our normalisation ensures preconditions for correlating stocks best as possible. Namely, we tested stationarity, data-distribution, homoscedasticity, structural breaks, autocorrelation, seasonality, and outliers. In our evaluation we saw only a few stocks failing some of the tests.

With all necessary statistical preconditions established, we calculate the pairwise cross-correlation between all normalised stock time series. For that, we use Pearson's r bivariate sample correlation coefficient. The average correlation between the 108,811 pairs of unprocessed stocks is very high with $r = 0.96$, but after pre-processing drops to a zero-centred normal distribution with $\sigma = 0.12$. Previously, we mentioned that the data can be normalised either with the average performance of stocks in one industry or the entire S&P 500 index. In our correlation analysis we only saw positive correlations with a median of $\tilde{r} = 0.2$ for market-wise normalisation. Because these correlations are not zero-centred, they are assumed to still have significant shared exogenous influences which pollute the individual correlation values. Concluding, the industry-wise normalisation, which ensures a zero-centred distribution, is preferable for removing exogenous influences.

We use the correlation factor as edge weights in the relationship graph. Different to the graph based on news, there are edges for all pairwise stocks.

5 Comparing Relationship Graphs from Stocks and News

In previous sections we described how we generate company relationship graphs from news and stocks with weighted edges describing the strength of relationship. With over 100k edges in the graph based on stocks and over 15k edges in the graph based on news, it is impossible to produce a meaningful visualisation. Therefore, we select only edges outside the respective 99.9th percentile in Fig. 2. For the news graph this leaves 90 edges between 98 nodes from all eleven industry sectors. For the stock graph this means we apply a threshold of $r = 0.368$ on the absolute correlation-based edge weights and are left with 109 edges among 123 different stocks from all industry sectors. A node's size is determined respectively to its total revenue in 2010 in order to indicate its importance, the colour coincides with the industry. The visualised graphs only consist of the most extreme values and might therefore not be representative for the entire graphs. However, by being the most extreme samples, this also means, that only the most certain relationships based on either type of data is shown.

Qualitative (Visual) Comparison. Comparing both graphs (visually), we see very different structures. Both graphs share 29 nodes and four edges only. Instead of many small decoupled sub-graphs for industry sectors the news graph reveals one big sub-graph consisting of 50 nodes from many different industry sectors. Some edges between companies sound comprehensible after investigating their business relationships. For example, *Microsoft Corp. (MSFT)* and *Viacom Inc.* announced a long-term strategic alliance for corporate segments like game development and advertisement in 2007. To mention another example, a high pairwise distance can be observed for both streaming providers *Netflix Inc. (NFLX)* and *Amazon.com Inc. (AMZN)* which both benefit from the increased demand in this segment of the market. Over the whole graph, only 28 edges are

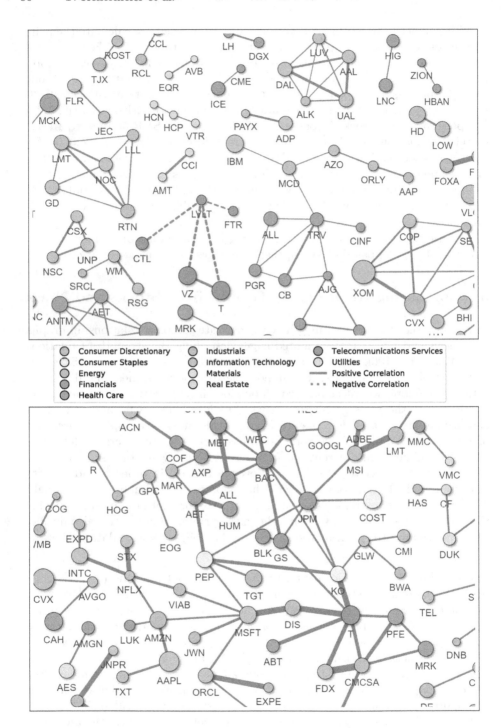

Fig. 2. Excerpts of relationship graphs based on stock similarity (top) and news articles (bottom). Only edges with weights above the 99.9th percentile are drawn.

connections among companies originating from the same industry. The greatest industry cluster can be observed for companies from the sector *Financials* which includes insurance companies (e.g. *American International Group, Inc.*), investment banks (e.g. *JPMorgan Chase & Co.*) and financial service providers (e.g. *Citigroup Inc.*). Some of them are densely connected with other industries which can be argued by their investments in stocks of other companies.

In the stock graph, a large proportion of high correlations are observed among companies belonging to the same industry sectors. Only eight edges between two different sectors are present in this visualisation. In terms of inter-industry connections, the node *MCD* (*McDonald's Corp.*) in the center of the graph is the strongest one since it is connected to nodes from three different industries. Investigation by financial news did not reveal an underlying relationship with the connected companies. Instead, this stock appears to be an appropriate strong representative component of the market performance and therefore is strongly linked to other important representative components like *IBM*. From the 109 edges selected for the graph, only four represent a negative correlation which all originate from the industry sector *Telecommunications Services*. Further, it should be noted that there a three companies for which each one compromises two stocks. Because two stocks of the same company are almost equal, these three correlation pairs reveal the highest r.

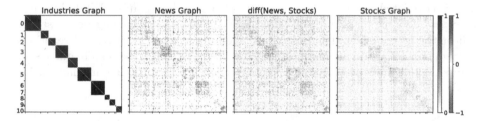

Fig. 3. Adjacency matrices for the industries graph, stocks graph, news graph and their difference. The industries graph contains only edges between companies of the same industry. The industry sectors are as follows (top to bottom): Consumer Discretionary; Consumer Staples; Energy; Financials; Health Care; Industrials; Information Technology; Materials; Real Estate; Telecommunications Services; Utilities

Quantitative Comparison. As denoted previously, the visualisations of the graphs are not entirely representable. The adjacency matrices in Fig. 3 reveal some overall patterns. The edges between companies from the same industry sectors are stronger for both graphs. For the stocks graph, the companies in the sector *Health Care* have a low correlation to companies from any other sectors. This pattern is still persistent after taking the difference of both graphs. Further, there are strong disagreements observable between both graphs regarding the sectors *Industrials*, *Information Technology* and *Utilities*. As already seen in the qualitative evaluation, the companies in the sector *Financials* usually have high edge weights with other companies in the news graph.

Table 1. Pearson's r for comparing graphs based on co-occurrence counts, minimum and pairwise distances in news with normalised and raw stock correlations

		News		
		Count	Min-Dist	Pairwise-Dist
Stocks	Normalised	0.0945	0.1124	**0.1284**
	Raw	–	–	−0.0037

In order to measure the compatibility of both graphs and their different variations, we conduct a comparison of the stock correlations and the extracted business relationships. The number of edges in the unfiltered graphs are incompatible for comparison. Thus, we use only companies and relations that appear in both graphs resulting in 417 companies and 86,736 unique bidirectional edges. We use the absolute correlation as weights in the stock graph and adjust the scale of edge weights. Table 1 shows the correlation of graphs weighted by different metrics. The graph of relationships extracted from news weighted by pairwise distances of company mentions in the texts has the highest similarity to the correlations between normalised stocks. The correlation graph of raw stock prices is expected to contain almost exclusively spurious correlations, but is included for comparison purposes. In the graph from raw stocks, almost all companies are highly correlated, hence the low similarity to all other graphs. While business news are dominated by reports about new alliances or financing deals, stocks reflect the actual effect that this has on the market and also investors reactions that go beyond what gets featured in news. This can clearly be seen in our visual comparison of most prevalent company relationships and also in our quantitative analysis.

6   Conclusions

In this work we have demonstrated two methods to create a graph of company relationships. We extracted company mentions from business news and proposed three approaches to add edge weights as an indicator of how strong a particular relation is. In our second approach, we extracted the company relationships from historic stock market data, for which we proposed extensive pre-processing steps to ensure that autoregressive and external influences do not invalidate the results. Based on four years historical stock prices and seven years financial news, we found evidence supporting the hypothesis that both graphs show similarities. However, we had to introduce limitations and assumptions, as business relationship and intrinsic value are not directly observable. Through the methods presented in this paper, we introduced proxies for these information in the form of weighted graphs. We examined how well a stock price can be described by stock prices of related companies to understand to what extent stock movements are determined by business relationships. As there is no complete collection of business relationships, we used co-occurrences of company mentions in news articles. In our evaluation, the edge weights based on pairwise distances are most similar to stock correlations.

We see a lot of potential use cases for company relationship graphs in downstream tasks, for example as additional information in entity embedding models, extending knowledge bases, or as a supporting feature in market analysis.

References

1. Akita, R., Yoshihara, A., Matsubara, T., Uehara, K.: Deep learning for stock prediction using numerical and textual information. In: International Conference on Computer and Information Science, pp. 1–6 (2016)
2. Bachelier, L.: Theory of speculation. In: Annales scientifiques de l'École normale supérieure (1900)
3. Box, G.E.P., Cox, D.R.: An analysis of transformations. J. R. Stat. Soc.: Ser. B (Methodol.) **26**, 211–243 (1964)
4. Box, G.E.P., Jenkins, G.M.: Time series analysis forecasting and control. J. Time Ser. Anal. (1970)
5. Chen, Y., Wei, Z., Huang, X.: Incorporating corporation relationship via graph convolutional neural networks for stock price prediction. In: Proceedings of the ACM International Conference on Information and Knowledge Management, pp. 1655–1658. ACM (2018)
6. Ding, X., Zhang, Y., Liu, T., Duan, J.: Using structured events to predict stock price movement: an empirical investigation. In: Proceedings of the Conference on Empirical Methods in Natural Language Processing, pp. 1415–1425 (2014)
7. Dionisio, A., Menezes, R., Mendes, D.A.: Mutual information: a measure of dependency for nonlinear time series. Phys. A: Stat. Mech. Appl. **344**, 326–329 (2004)
8. Engle, R.F., Granger, C.W.J.: Co-integration and error correction: representation, estimation, and testing. Econometrica **55**, 251–276 (1987)
9. Fama, E.F.: Random walks in stock market prices. Financ. Anal. J. **21**, 55–59 (1965)
10. Fleming, J., Ostdiek, B., Whaley, R.E.: Predicting stock market volatility: a new measure. J. Future Mark. **15**, 265–302 (1995)
11. Franke, J., Härdle, W.K., Hafner, C.M.: Statistics of Financial Markets (2010)
12. Granger, C.W.J.: Investigating causal relations by econometric models and cross-spectral methods. Econometrica **37**, 424–438 (1969)
13. Granger, C.W.J., Newbold, P.: Spurious regressions in econometrics. J. Econ. **2**, 111–120 (1974)
14. Hallin, M.: Gauss-Markov Theorem in Statistics. Wiley (2006). ISBN 9781118445112
15. Hong, H., et al.: Trading and Returns Under Periodic Market Closures (1998)
16. Hsu, M.W., Lessmann, S., Sung, M.C., Ma, T., Johnson, J.E.: Bridging the divide in financial market forecasting: machine learners vs. financial economists. Expert Syst. Appl. **61**, 215–234 (2016)
17. Khadjeh Nassirtoussi, A., Aghabozorgi, S., Ying Wah, T., Ngo, D.C.L.: Text mining of news-headlines for FOREX market prediction: a multi-layer dimension reduction algorithm with semantics and sentiment. Expert Syst. Appl. **42**, 306–324 (2015)

18. Khadjeh Nassirtoussi, A., Aghabozorgi, S., Wah, T., Ngo, D.: Text mining for market prediction: a systematic review. Expert Syst. Appl. **41**, 7653–7670 (2014)
19. Kim, S.: A cross-correlation-based stock forecasting model. In: Proceedings of The National Conference On Undergraduate Research (2016)
20. Kosapattarapim, C.: Granger causality between stock prices and currency exchange rates in Thailand. In: AIP Conference Proceedings, vol. 1905, p. 50025, March 2017
21. Lee, H., Surdeanu, M., MacCartney, B., Jurafsky, D.: On the importance of text analysis for stock price prediction. In: Proceedings of the Language Resources and Evaluation Conference, pp. 1170–1175 (2014)
22. Li, B., Chan, K.C., Ou, C., Ruifeng, S.: Discovering public sentiment in social media for predicting stock movement of publicly listed companies. Inf. Syst. **69**, 81–92 (2017)
23. Li, X., Xie, H., Chen, L., Wang, J., Deng, X.: News impact on stock price return via sentiment analysis. Knowl.-Based Syst. **69**, 14–23 (2014)
24. Lipenkova, J.: A system for fine-grained aspect-based sentiment analysis of Chinese. In: ACL-IJCNLP, pp. 55–60. ACL (2015)
25. Millo, G.: Robust standard error estimators for panel models: a unifying approach. J. Stat. Softw. **82**, 1–27 (2017)
26. Morgan, I.G.: Stock prices and heteroscedasticity. J. Bus. **49**, 496–508 (1976)
27. Peng, Y., Jiang, H.: Leverage financial news to predict stock price movements using word embeddings and deep neural networks. In: Annual Conference of the North American Chapter of the Association for Computational Linguistics: Human Language Technologies (2016)
28. Lopez de Prado, M.: Advances in Financial Machine Learning. Wiley, Hoboken (2018)
29. Ruiz, E.J., Hristidis, V., Castillo, C., Gionis, A., Jaimes, A.: Correlating financial time series with micro-blogging activity. In: Proceedings of the Fifth ACM International Conference on Web Search and Data Mining. ACM (2012)
30. Sun, A., Lachanski, M., Fabozzi, F.J.: Trade the tweet: social media text mining and sparse matrix factorization for stock market prediction. Int. Rev. Financ. Anal. **48**, 272–281 (2016)
31. Vlastakis, N., Markellos, R.N.: Information demand and stock market volatility. J. Bank. Finance **36**, 1808–1821 (2012)
32. Wang, F., Shieh, S.J., Havlin, S., Stanley, H.E.: Statistical analysis of the overnight and daytime return. Phys. Rev. E **79**, 056109 (2009)
33. Yule, G.U.: Why do we sometimes get nonsense-correlations between Time-Series?- a study in sampling and the nature of time-series. J. R. Stat. Soc. **89**, 1–63 (1926)
34. Zhai, Y., Hsu, A., Halgamuge, S.K.: Combining news and technical indicators in daily stock price trends prediction. In: Liu, D., Fei, S., Hou, Z., Zhang, H., Sun, C. (eds.) ISNN 2007. LNCS, vol. 4493, pp. 1087–1096. Springer, Heidelberg (2007). https://doi.org/10.1007/978-3-540-72395-0_132

Mining Financial Risk Events from News and Assessing their Impact on Stocks

Saumya Bhadani, Ishan Verma(✉), and Lipika Dey

TCS Innovation Labs, Tata Consultancy Services, New Delhi, India
{saumya.bhadani,ishan.verma,lipika.dey}@tcs.com

Abstract. The impact of financial risk events on stock market is a fairly established area of research in the financial domain. However, the analysts require these events to be represented in a structured form in order to carry out statistical analysis. In this work, we aim is to identify and extract various financial risk events from news articles along with associated organizations to facilitate integrated analysis with structured business data. We propose a two-phase risk extraction algorithm involving a CNN based semi-supervised risk event identification and gradient boosting based entity association algorithm to extract risk events from news and associate them to their target organizations. We have analyzed large volumes of past available data using Granger causality to assess the impact of these events on various stock indices. Further, the utility of extracted risk events in predicting stock movement has been shown using a Bi-LSTM network based prediction model. The proposed system outperforms state of the art linear SVM on data for different stock indices.

Keywords: Financial risk mining · Information extraction · Granger causality · Gradient boosting · Predictive analytics

1 Introduction

Enterprise risk refers to certain conditions or situations which may give rise to negative implications. It is the possibility of an event that may affect the growth and profitability of an organization [16]. Incorporating different types of risk associated with organizations plays an integral role in any financial analysis. Organizations are always exposed to various risk events like credit rating downgrade, recession, quarterly loss, customer behaviour changes, or business policy changes that can dramatically affect their yield or their operating model or mode of conducting business. Therefore, any tool capable of capturing unanticipated risk factors carries significant potential value. The risk elements can have both structured and unstructured factors. The financial reports published by an organization are a good source of structured risk factors like profit margins, growth percentage, revenue etc. However, the unstructured risk factors are more textual in nature and often expressed in natural language form like Merger & Acquisition, CEO change, competitor profile etc. These unstructured risks factors are

© Springer Nature Switzerland AG 2020
V. Bitetta et al. (Eds.): MIDAS 2019, LNAI 11985, pp. 85–100, 2020.
https://doi.org/10.1007/978-3-030-37720-5_7

Fig. 1. Sample risk event

usually identified from external sources like news, social media, analyst reports etc. Figure 1 shows "quarterly loss" risk event reported for "Axis Bank".

Any risk mitigation and management activity need to address both structured and unstructured risk elements at the same time. While literature exists on various methods to incorporate structured risk elements, the challenge lies in quantifying the unstructured risk elements due to their non-numeric domain. The job of an expert analyst is to sweep through large volumes of text data like news, social media, market reports etc. to identify and quantify these qualitative risk elements. Apart from the identification of the risk elements, it is also important to identify the associated organizations with each risk element. Both the organization and the corresponding risk factor can then be used to perform an overall risk analysis of different portfolio or the industry sector as a whole. Risk event detection from news is a challenging task due to the volume, velocity and variety of digital news content that gets published round the clock. It becomes extremely difficult for a person or a group of persons to manually sweep through this vast data, thereby giving rise to the need of intelligent systems that can sift through the content and detect the risk events automatically. In this work, we propose a risk event detection and classification system to automatically detect and categorize risk events from news sources. This system is trained using deep neural nets. These risk events often mention multiple entities with different roles in the context of a single event. We also propose a gradient-boosting based method that can disambiguate among these entities using linguistic features and correctly identify the target of the risk event. Moreover, we have used Granger causality to assess the impact of these events on different stock indices. A Bidirectional Long-short term network (Bi-LSTM) based machine learning model has been used to predict stock movement direction based on the risk events reported in news along with historical stock data.

The rest of the paper is organized as follows. Section 2 presents related works in the area of risk information extraction from text documents and their applications. Section 3 details the risk event extraction. Section 4 presents a methodology to assess the impact of risk events on stock movement direction and Sect. 5 explains the algorithm for stock movement prediction. Experimental Results are presented in Sect. 6. Section 7 concludes the paper with a brief touch upon future work.

2 Related Work

There has been a fairly large body of work on event extraction from text data. Though risk event extraction has not been in limelight, researchers have continuously proposed work in this area. To limit the scope of the related work, a summary has been presented on various work done in the area of risk extraction from text and its varied applications. Several management approaches have been proposed to mitigate a wide variety of risk factors associated with an enterprise [6,13]. However, majority of those studies incorporated risk assessment using structured risk factors and very few previous studies have addressed the problem of identifying risk from unstructured data like news articles, social media, and analyst reports. Kogan et al. [5] studied the correlation between enterprise risk mentions and share price volatility. The authors have used SEC 10K filings and a set of human identified trigger words. A regression model using document-level unigram features was proposed to predict volatility in stock movement. Lu and Hung [10] presented a framework for annotating organization specific risk statements. News articles from the Wall Street Journal were taken and manually annotated to verify the framework. The framework used the simplistic bag-of-words model as features along with SVM to train and classify risk related texts into good or bad risks. Leidner and Schilder [8] have described and implemented a system comprising an offline risk taxonomy miner, an online risk alert and a visualization component which have been applied to earnings call transcripts. Their work aimed to find risk-indicative words and phrases automatically. The authors have combined Web mining and Information Extraction techniques to detect enterprise risks automatically before they materialize, thus providing valuable business intelligence. Dasgupta et al. [1] presented a framework that processes human-reported risk descriptions to classify them into true risk and false alarm categories. The authors used SVM with different linguistic features to automatically identify and label text descriptions as valid and invalid risks. Nugent and Leidner [12] proposed a supervised learning approach that combines a weakly-supervised risk taxonomy, named entity tagging and dependency tree analysis to perform company-risk relationship classification. The work also demonstrates that SVM with a tree kernel, trained on hand-annotated news articles is capable of outperforming a selection of alternative classification algorithms. Satoh and Samejima [15] presented an approach for risk word suggestion for making a risk auditor aware of potential risks based on words of identified risks in an audit report. Words of potential risks are suggested to the auditor based on the auditors' description of identified risks.

Wang and Hua [19] proposed a text regression system where given the transcript of an earnings call, their regression model predicted the volatility of stock prices from the week after the call is made. Tsai and Wang [17] attempted to utilize text information in financial reports to analyze financial risk among companies. Their work studied the relation between financial sentiments and financial risk by utilizing a finance-specific sentiment dictionary. They showed that financial sentiment word-based model has performance comparable to a whole text model.

The key distinguishable feature of our work is that it does not require human-identified risk words and is capable of detecting new types of risk events reported in text sources. Based on the methods exploited by earlier authors for risk extraction, we have chosen a SVM based classifier as our baseline for risk identification. We show that the proposed method outperforms the baseline by a fair margin. Experiments have also been conducted to show the utility of quantification of risk events in term of Granger causality tests and prediction of stock movement.

3   Risk Event Extraction

We have built a two-stage risk event extraction algorithm. In the first stage, we determine the risk events from financial news articles and in the second stage, we identify the target entities (companies or industrial sectors) which are affected by the risks. We employ Convolutional Neural Network (CNN) based classifier to identify the "risk" sentences from the news articles, and then for the "risk" sentences, we determine the main keyword which had the highest contribution towards the risk class using a weakly supervised learning method based on the CNN. These risk words are utilized in the second stage, where we first recognize the entity (company and industrial sector) names and then identify the entities affected by the risk using a relation classifier.

3.1   Risk Sentence Classification with Word Localization

We have utilized Convolutional Neural Network (CNN) to classify the sentences into two classes, "risk" and "not risk", and to determine the main keyword which signifies the risk in case of a "risk" classification. The network architecture is based on the CNN model which was first proposed for text classification by Kim

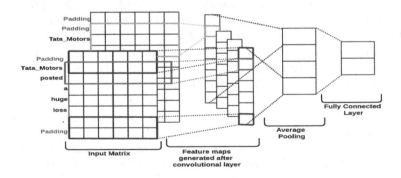

Fig. 2. CNN architecture

in [4], and is demonstrated in Fig. 2. However, the network in [4] only determined the class of the text input and did not identify the main word or phrase which had the highest contribution towards the classification. We need to determine the main keyword for the risk classification, as it would be further utilized to determine the affected entities. As the training data does not explicitly have any word or phrase level information, we employed a weakly supervised learning method based on the CNN.

In [7], the authors have proposed a CNN network architecture, which determines the sentiment of text sentences, and also identifies the crucial word which is responsible for the particular sentiment, using a weakly supervised learning method. We have also applied a similar method for our risk event extraction.

In the proposed model demonstrated in Fig. 2, words of the sentences are embedded in a fixed size of continuous vector space using GloVe word embedding [14] and then they are concatenated to form the initial input matrix of the CNN. Zero padding is added so that each word would be included in the receptive field the same number of times, irrespective of the word's position. Along with the zero padding, the dimension of the input matrix X is $[d+2(h-1)]$, where k, d and h represent the dimension of word embedding vector, maximum length of a sentence and height of the receptive field respectively.

$$\mathrm{X} = \mathrm{x}_{1:l} = 0_{1:(h-1)} \odot \mathrm{x}_{1:d} \odot 0_{1:(h-1)} \tag{1}$$

Here $\odot$ represents concatenation. CNN performs convolution operation on the input matrix to create feature maps. In the convolution operation, a *filter* w with dimension of $h \times k$, is applied to each possible window of words in a particular sentence. The i-th feature map f_i is a I-dimensional vector, where I is $(d+h-1)$.

$$\mathrm{f_i} = [f_{1i}, f_{2i}, \ldots, f_{li}]^T, \tag{2}$$

$$f_{ji} = ReLu(\mathrm{w} \cdot \mathrm{x}_{j:j+h-1} + b), \tag{3}$$

$$\mathrm{w} \in R^{h \times k}, b \in R. \tag{4}$$

Here b is the bias term. For a given sentence, n feature maps are created where n is n_{ftypes} (the number of filter type) $\times$ $n_{filters}$ (the number of filters for each type). n_{ftypes} and $n_{filters}$ are provided as input arguments. Let $\hat{f}_l$ be the scalar value generated after applying average pooling to a particular feature map f_i. The n-dimensional feature vector z which is passed to the fully connected layer is:

$$z = [\hat{f}_1, \hat{f}_2, \ldots, \hat{f}_n] \tag{5}$$

And finally, the output y of a fully connected layer is:

$$y = \mathrm{W}_{fc} \cdot \mathrm{z} + \mathrm{b}_{fc}, \tag{6}$$

$$\mathrm{W}_{fc} \in R^{c \times n}, \tag{7}$$

$$b \in R^c. \tag{8}$$

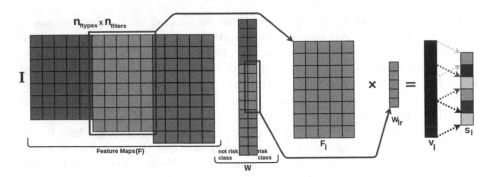

Fig. 3. Computing the score vector using feature maps and weights of the fully connected layer in CNN.

where W_{fc} is the weight matrix for the fully connected layer, b_{fc} is the bias term and c is the number of classes.

Now, to determine the risk key word, we calculate a score vector which contains the importance score of each word in the sentence. This score vector is generated by combining the weights of the fully connected layer with the feature maps as shown in Fig. 3. Let F_l be the concatenation of all the feature maps f_i, for the l-th filter type, and w_{lr} be the row vector of W_{fc} for the l-th filter type and the "risk" class. The score vector for l-th filter type is calculated as follows:

$$v_l = F_l \cdot w_{lr}^T \tag{9}$$

$$F_l \in R^{I \times n_{filters}} \tag{10}$$

$$w_{lr} \in R^{n_{filters}} \tag{11}$$

However, v_l does not signify the scores for single token of words, but for the combination of h subsequent tokens. The d-dimensional score vector whose each element corresponds to each word, is obtained by averaging h elements of v_l with step size of 1.

$$s_l = \left\{ e_p | e_p = \frac{1}{h} \sum_{q=p}^{p+h-1} v_{l_p} \right\} \tag{12}$$

s_l is a d-dimensional vector for all filter types, irrespective of the value of h. To get the final score vector s, we can simple add the s_l of each filter type.

$$s = \sum_{l=1}^{n_{ftype}} s_l \tag{13}$$

Now, the word having the highest score is selected as representative "risk" keyword.

$$\alpha = \max(\mathbf{s})$$
$$K = \{w_i | s_i = \alpha\} \tag{14}$$

All the words in the set K have highest importance score and thus any word can be randomly picked from K, as the main risk keyword for the particular sentence, and can be used to determine the target affected entities using the relation classifier. However, during our experiments, in almost all cases, K consisted of one word.

3.2 Entity Recognition and Disambiguation

To determine the entities affected by the risk events, we initially need to identify and disambiguate all the entities in a news document. We use Stanford NER [2] which recognizes named entities as well as categorizes them as organization, location or person among several other categories. Spacy's neuralcoref[1] module is utilized for co-reference resolution. After co-reference resolution, the references to entities are replaced by the corresponding entity names in the news content. To disambiguate the company names, we use the DBpedia Spotlight tool [11]. Spotlight tool annotates each entity recognized by the Stanford NER, with a unique identifier and the entities which refer to the same organization, person or location will have the same identifier. Additionally, modified title and content of the news documents are constructed, with the entities replaced by their spotlight identifiers. For example, "TCS", "Tata Consultancy Services" and "TCS Ltd" refer to the same entity and spotlight returns "Tata_Consultancy_Services" identifier for all of them.

However, the industrial sector names such as "Banking sector" or "IT sector" are not recognized by the Stanford NER and to identify and disambiguate them, we use a keyword based approach. We track only a selected number of industrial sectors, including "Auto", "Banking", "IT", "Pharmaceutical" etc. For each of these sectors, we prepared a list of keywords frequently used as their alternatives. Whenever these keywords appeared in the content and were followed by the words, "sector" or "industry", they were tagged and also resolved. For example, the words "IT sector", "IT industry", "Information Technology industry" will all be resolved to "Information_Technology_Sector". After resolution, the references to the sectors are replaced by the corresponding resolved name in the news title and content.

3.3 Target Entity Identification

Once the "risk" sentences and their corresponding key risk word is detected, we identify the entities, which constitute companies and industrial sectors, which are likely to be affected by the risk event. We accomplish this task through a relation classifier. Table 1 shows examples of text snippets, with risk keywords detected by the CNN text classifier, and entity names appearing in their proximity highlighted in bold, and also presents the inferences drawn by the domain experts. The purpose of the relation classifier is to judge the correctness of risk keyword-entity pairs for a given text snippet containing a risk keyword and an

---

[1] https://spacy.io/universe/project/neuralcoref.

Table 1. Examples of text snippets with risk keyword and co-occurring entities along with human inferences for Risk-Entity association

Text snippets	Human inference
Policy advisers are worried that the global **slowdown** could hurt the manufacturing sector—hitting **Auto_Sector**, engineering, textile and some other labour intensive sectors	Auto_Sector is at risk
Added to this, the IL& FS woes have led to a liquidity **crunch** across much of the shadow **Banking_Sector** and throttled off some lending	Banking_Sector is at a risk of liquidity crunch
The price war launched by **Jio** has led to **attrition** of customers from both **Idea** and **Vodafone**	Idea and Vodafone are at risk due to competition from Jio
In the March quarter, when competitors such as **SpiceJet** and **Indigo** had posted post-tax profits, **Jet_Airways** reported a **loss** of Rs 1,036 crore	Only Jet_Airways reported a loss, not SpiceJet or Indigo

entity in the proximity of the risk keyword, where correctness implies the judgement of correct target entity for an identified risk.

This problem has been formulated as a binary classification problem where given a risk keyword, an entity and their corresponding text snippet, the task is to classify this sample into {0,1}, where 1 represents that the entity is the target entity for the given risk and 0 specifies that the given entity is not the risk target.

The entity mentions in a given text snippet are replaced with placeholders where the target entity name is replaced by one placeholder and all the other entity names are replaced with another placeholder. Multiple text-specific morphological and dependency features are extracted from the modified text snippet to create a feature vector for the classification task. The risk keyword and the entity play a prominent part in the feature vector generation. To create the feature vector, we first determine the Term Frequency-Inverse Document Frequency (*tf-idf*) feature vector representation for the text snippet. Next, we determine the dependency relation between the entity and risk keyword and calculate the shortest chain of dependencies between them. The dependencies appearing in the shortest chain are encoded as binary vector similar to bag-of-words representation. The vocabulary of all dependencies are first constructed and the dependencies obtained for a text snippet are set to 1, in the shortest dependency relations vector. For example, for the statement "Axis_Bank posts a loss", the shortest dependency path between "Axis_Bank" and "loss" is ("nsubj","dobj") and in the dependency path vector, the value corresponding to "nsubj" and "dobj" are set to 1 and rest are set to 0. This vector is then appended to the *tf-idf* vector representation of the snippet. Finally, the length of the shortest chain of dependencies is also appended.

Using the above-mentioned feature vector as input, we have used Naive Bayes (NB) and Support Vector Machine (SVM) with linear kernel to create a baseline for the classification task and conducted experiments using Random Forest [9] and Gradient Boosted Trees [3] ensemble classifiers. Grid search was used to find the best hyper-parameters for each algorithm. In our experiments, GBT gave the best results which are elucidated in Sect. 6. Therefore we employed GBT as the relation classifier. As the output of the relation classifier, we obtain the target entities (company or industrial sectors) for the risk events detected by the CNN.

Through the risk event extraction system, for each news article, we obtain the risk events represented by the risk keyword (detected by CNN), and the target affected company or industrial sector. Therefore, for a particular company or industrial sector, all the risk events obtained from news articles can be aggregated for a day or week or month. A time-series representing the risk events can further be obtained for the company or the industrial sector. For the broad market indexes (like Nifty50, Nifty100, etc), the time-stamped risk events of all the member companies can be collected to define the risk time-series of the whole Index. Similarly, for the sectoral indexes (Nifty Bank, Nifty Auto, etc) the risk events of the corresponding industrial sector and the member companies can be collected to define the risk time-series. In this way, the risk time-series of a single company, Sectoral Index and Market Index can be formulated for various intervals, and utilized in the prediction of stock values.

4   Assessing Impact of Risk Events

To assess the impact of identified risk events on stock indices, we chose to use Granger causality test. The Granger causality test is a statistical hypothesis test for determining whether a time-series X is useful in forecasting another time-series Y. X is accepted as impacting Y, if and only if, prediction of future values of Y improves after considering values of X. The idea is to investigate whether daily occurrences of risk events encoded as a time-series helps predict future stock movement direction.

$$y_t = \alpha + \sum_{i=1}^{n} \beta_i y_{t-i} + \varepsilon_t \tag{15}$$

$$y_t = \alpha + \sum_{i=1}^{n} \beta_i y_{t-i} + \sum_{i=1}^{n} \gamma_i x_{t-i} + \varepsilon_t \tag{16}$$

In Eq. 15 future values of Y are predicted using its past values. Equation 16 predicts future values of Y using past values of both X and Y.

In our case X is binary risk event occurrence time series with granularity of a single day where 1 denotes occurrence and 0 denotes absence of a risk event. The time span of impact of news event on stock movement is still a debate amongst researchers. Past studies do not show a consensus on a fixed time window in which the impact of events can be observed. Accordingly, we have experimented with different sets of time-delays ranging over 1, 3, and 5 days.

For Granger causality test, the p-value for rejecting the null hypothesis is set to 5%. This means that if the p-value is observed to be less than 5% then it can be safely assumed that X Granger-causes Y.

We conducted the Granger causality test between various broad market and sectoral indices of the Indian stock exchange and risk events. Experimental results are presented in Sect. 6.2. The impact of risk events is not identical for different sectors. Our results support this view.

5   Stock Movement Prediction

Stock movement prediction of indexes can be formulated as a binary-valued prediction problem resulting in whether the stock will rise or fall. We have utilized the risk events extracted by our risk event detection algorithm, along with the previous stock values to address this problem.

We input the encoded risk events and stock values for a specific time interval in LSTM and Bi-directional LSTM networks, which predict whether the stock will fall or rise in the future. LSTM and Bi-LSTM are types of Recurrent Neural Networks and are known to be useful in solving time-series prediction problems. The hidden state of LSTM considers information from only previous time steps, while the hidden state of Bi-LSTM considers information from both directions. We have used the vanilla LSTM and Bi-LSTM models without any change in the model parameters.

The input to the prediction model was created as a fixed valued risk vector for each day. We first analyzed all the risk keywords detected by CNN on the whole dataset and extracted the top 40 risk words that occurred most frequently. This set constituted words like "loss", "downgrade", "bankruptcy", "debt" etc, and are used as our risk vocabulary. If for a particular day, CNN detected the keyword which belonged to the risk vocabulary, the value of the keyword index was set to 1 in the risk vector. If the keyword did not belong to the risk vocabulary, we calculated the cosine similarity of that keyword with all the words in the risk vocabulary using the GloVe word embeddings, and if the similarity with a particular vocabulary word was greater than a threshold then the index of that word was set to 1 in the risk vector.

For example, for a particular day, the CNN identified, "distressed" and "insolvency" as risk keywords. Since the word "distressed" belonged to the risk vocabulary, in the risk vector, the value corresponding to the index of "distressed" is set to 1. However "insolvency" is not a part of the vocabulary, and thus the cosine similarity of "insolvency" is calculated with all the risk words in the vocabulary. The similarity of "bankruptcy" and "insolvency" is greater than a threshold, thus the value corresponding to the index of "bankruptcy" is set to 1 in the risk vector. If a keyword is not similar to any risk vocabulary words, it is ignored. In this way we created a risk vector of length 40 for each day, corresponding to a company, sectoral index or broad market index.

We used the risk vector in conjunction with the stock values to predict the rise or fall of the stock. For each day, we concatenated the risk vector of a company or index with their stock value to create the input vector. We considered the time intervals of 1 day, 3 days and 1 week. The input vectors for each day in the time interval was sequentially sent to the prediction model, and they were used to predict the rise or fall of the stock for the next day.

6   Experiments and Evaluations

6.1   Data Description

A news repository has been built from news documents collected from Moneycontrol.com business news section.[2] Moneycontrol.com is one of the largest online financial platforms in India. The repository contains over 38000 documents collected for the duration of Oct-2011 to Mar-2019. To prepare the dataset for risk sentence classification, we extracted around 7000 random sentences from the repository and sent them to the domain experts, who manually classified 2975 sentences as "risk" sentences. The rest were marked as "non-risk". There was no explicit marking of risk words in the annotated dataset. We used 70% of the data for training, 10% for validation and 20% for testing. The entire dataset has been used for the Granger causality test. However, evaluation of the prediction task is done using temporal data split where data from Oct-2011 to Dec-2016 are used for training and the data from Jan-2017 to Mar-2019 have been used for testing.

Indexes considered for evaluation: A stock market index is created by selecting a group of stocks that are representative of the whole market or a specified sector or segment of the market. In this work, we have chosen NIFTY 50 as the broad market index and NIFTY AUTO and NIFTY BANK as the sectoral indices from the Indian stock market to carry out our experiments. The NIFTY 50 is a diversified 50 stock index accounting for 13 sectors of the economy. NIFTY Auto and NIFTY Bank represent the performance of Indian automobile and banking industry respectively.

Evaluations: Our experiments are carried out on three different time intervals: 1 day, 3 days and a week. We test the influence of risk events in predicting the polarity of stock indices movement for each time interval. Our feature set includes daily risk event occurrences and previous days stock indices values.

We have chosen accuracy and Matthews Correlation Coefficient (MCC) as two assessment metrics to evaluate the performance of the prediction algorithm. MCC acts as a balanced measure which can be used even if the classes are of very different sizes. MCC ranges between -1 and $+1$. A coefficient of $+1$ represents a perfect prediction, 0 no better than random prediction and -1 indicates total disagreement between prediction and observation. MCC is computed as follows:

$$MCC = \frac{(tp * tn)(fp * fn)}{\sqrt{(tp + fp)(tp + fn)(tn + fp)(tn + fn)}} \tag{17}$$

---

[2] https://www.moneycontrol.com/news/business/.

Table 2. Evaluations of classifiers for risk sentence classification

Classifier	Precision	Recall	F measure	Accuracy
SVM with *tf-idf*	0.56	0.75	0.64	0.74
Gradient Boosting	0.80	0.78	0.76	0.77
CNN	0.80	0.77	0.78	0.81

where tp, tn, fp and fn are True Positive, False Positive, True Negative and False Negative, respectively.

6.2 Results

Risk Extraction Results: Table 2 demonstrates the classification performance of our models. For the baseline method, we represented the sentences using *tf-idf*, and then classified them using SVM and Gradient Boosted Trees Classifier. It can be seen that CNN performed the best among these. Moreover, word localization capability of CNN acts as an input to the target entity organization algorithm.

For training and evaluating our relation classifier for Target Entity Identification module, we took a subset of expert marked risk sentences containing at least one co-occurring entity from the dataset that we had created earlier. The central idea was to create a dataset of risk events with entity mentions such that both target and non-target entities are present in the training samples. Out of these 1000 risk event-entity relation samples, 408 samples were classified as 1 and 592 were classified as 0. Experimental results for the task of target entity identification with multiple machine learning algorithms on 80:20 train-test split are shown in Table 3. As stated earlier, Gradient Boosting has the best precision, recall, F1-score and accuracy and thus, we have utilized Gradient Boosting based relation classifier in our system.

Granger Causality Results: Figure 4 shows Granger causality result across different stock indices and risk events for all quarters ranging from Oct-2011 to Mar-2019. The chart shows $(1 - p)$ values for 1 day, 3 days and week time-lag plotted against each quarter for better interpretation of the results. The chart shows results for Nifty 50, Nifty Auto and Nifty Bank indices. The line of

Table 3. Evaluation of relation classifiers for target entity identification

Classifier	Precision	Recall	F measure	Accuracy
Naive Bayes	0.74	0.74	0.74	0.75
SVM	0.81	0.81	0.81	0.81
Random Forest	0.80	0.79	0.78	0.79
Gradient Boosting	0.82	0.82	0.82	0.83

significance is marked with yellow and it can be seen that on multiple occasions risk event granger causes stock movement changes across multiple stock market indices. However, several instances are there when there is no causality between the two. During our analysis, it was found that these non-causal periods have very less mention of risk events in news articles. Based on these results it can be seen that on multiple occasions, risk events extracted from news article play a role in stock market movement.

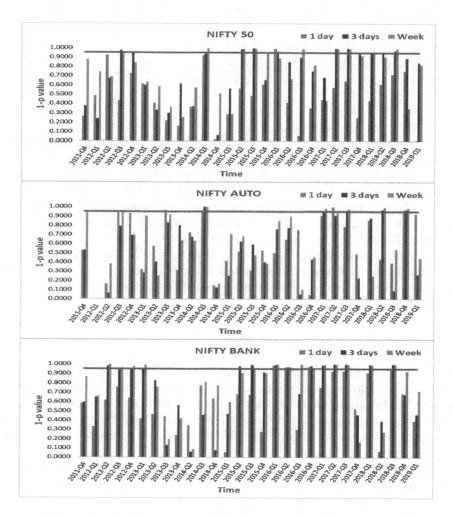

Fig. 4. Granger causality results for various indices

Prediction Results: Table 4 shows prediction results in the form of accuracy and MCC values for various prediction models. As stated earlier we have compared our results with SVM with linear kernel for the prediction task. It can be observed that the maximum accuracy achieved across all models for different

Table 4. Stock index movement prediction results

Index	No. of days	SVM		LSTM		BiLSTM	
		Accuracy	MCC	Accuracy	MCC	Accuracy	MCC
Nifty 50	1	0.60	0.03	0.44	0.07	0.44	0.07
	3	0.62	0.14	0.54	0.12	0.547	0.09
	5	0.60	0.13	0.55	0.15	0.58	0.10
Nifty bank	1	0.59	0.05	0.54	0.08	0.55	0.02
	3	0.59	0.11	0.59	0.22	0.58	0.18
	5	0.58	0.14	0.60	0.18	0.61	0.15
Nifty auto	1	0.54	0.08	0.51	0.02	0.51	0.018
	3	0.56	0.12	0.55	0.15	0.57	0.13
	5	0.58	0.15	0.56	0.17	0.565	0.17

indices is around 60%. Also, stocks movement are influenced by a multitude of other factors, thereby explaining the accuracy confinement in 50–60% zone. Both LSTM and Bi-LSTM outperforms SVM's in most of the cases for 3 day and week predictions. However, the same cannot be said for next day predictions where SVM performs better. A probable reason can be the absence of Granger causality which we saw in the earlier results. It is also interesting to observe that LSTM and Bi-LSTM accuracy always improves for longer time interval predictions.

The daily and weekly accuracy achieved using LSTM and Bi-LSTM based algorithm is comparable with prediction accuracy reported by Verma et al. [18] who also worked on predicting stock movement direction for various Indian stock market indices.

7   Conclusion and Future Work

Current work proposes a methodology for extracting risk events from unstructured sources. The proposed work makes use of news articles captured from the web to identify various financial risk events along with associated organizations. A CNN based approach to classify sentences and identify the main risk keyword from news articles is proposed. Each risk event is then associated with one or more organizations of possible impact using a gradient boosting based relation classifier along with syntactic dependency features. Granger causality tests have been carried out to obtain the impact of risk events on various Indian stock market indices. Also, the utility of capturing and quantifying risk event has been shown through an improvement in the prediction of stock by employing a Bi-LSTM based deep neural network prediction model. Experimental results verify that the inclusion of risk event can prove to be useful in stock data prediction. In future, the aim is to work towards more generic representations of risk events in terms of the numerical vector to facilitate deep understanding of the concept. Also, the impact of an individual risk event is still open research which we intend to work soon.

References

1. Dasgupta, T., Dey, L., Dey, P., Saha, R.: A framework for mining enterprise risk and risk factors from news documents. In: Proceedings of COLING 2016, the 26th International Conference on Computational Linguistics: System Demonstrations, pp. 180–184 (2016)
2. Finkel, J.R., Grenager, T., Manning, C.: Incorporating non-local information into information extraction systems by Gibbs sampling. In: Proceedings of the 43rd Annual Meeting on Association for Computational Linguistics, pp. 363–370. Association for Computational Linguistics (2005)
3. Friedman, J.H.: Greedy function approximation: a gradient boosting machine. Ann. Stat. **25**, 1189–1232 (2001)
4. Kim, Y.: Convolutional neural networks for sentence classification. In: Proceedings of the 2014 Conference on Empirical Methods in Natural Language Processing (EMNLP), pp. 1746–1751. Association for Computational Linguistics, October 2014
5. Kogan, S., Levin, D., Routledge, B.R., Sagi, J.S., Smith, N.A.: Predicting risk from financial reports with regression. In: Proceedings of Human Language Technologies: The 2009 Annual Conference of the North American Chapter of the Association for Computational Linguistics, pp. 272–280. Association for Computational Linguistics (2009)
6. Lam, J.: Enterprise Risk Management: From Incentives to Controls. Wiley, Hoboken (2014)
7. Lee, G., Jeong, J., Seo, S., Kim, C., Kang, P.: Sentiment classification with word localization based on weakly supervised learning with a convolutional neural network. Knowl.-Based Syst. **152**, 70–82 (2018)
8. Leidner, J.L., Schilder, F.: Hunting for the black swan: risk mining from text. In: Proceedings of the ACL 2010 System Demonstrations, pp. 54–59. Association for Computational Linguistics (2010)
9. Liaw, A., Wiener, M., et al.: Classification and regression by randomforest. R News **2**(3), 18–22 (2002)
10. Lu, H.-M., Huang, N.W.H., Zhang, Z., Chen, T.-J.: Identifying firm-specific risk statements in news articles. In: Chen, H., Yang, C.C., Chau, M., Li, S.-II. (eds.) PAISI 2009. LNCS, vol. 5477, pp. 42–53. Springer, Heidelberg (2009). https://doi.org/10.1007/978-3-642-01393-5_6
11. Mendes, P., Jakob, M., García-Silva, A., Bizer, C.: DBpedia spotlight: shedding light on the web of documents, pp. 1–8, September 2011
12. Nugent, T., Leidner, J.L.: Risk mining: company-risk identification from unstructured sources. In: 2016 IEEE 16th International Conference on Data Mining Workshops (ICDMW), pp. 1308–1311. IEEE (2016)
13. Olson, D.L., Wu, D.D.: Enterprise risk management, vol. 3. World Scientific Publishing Company (2015)
14. Pennington, J., Socher, R., Manning, C.D.: Glove: global vectors for word representation. EMNLP **14**, 1532–1543 (2014)
15. Satoh, N., Samejima, M.: Risk words suggestion for information security audit by Bayesian inference. Electron. Commun. Jpn. **102**(1), 42–48 (2019)
16. Taleb, N.N.: The Black Swan: The Impact of the Highly Improbable, vol. 2. Random House, New York City (2007)
17. Tsai, M.F., Wang, C.J.: On the risk prediction and analysis of soft information in finance reports. Eur. J. Oper. Res. **257**(1), 243–250 (2017)

18. Verma, I., Dey, L., Meisheri, H.: Detecting, quantifying and accessing impact of news events on Indian stock indices. In: Proceedings of the International Conference on Web Intelligence, pp. 550–557. ACM (2017)
19. Wang, W.Y., Hua, Z.: A semiparametric Gaussian copula regression model for predicting financial risks from earnings calls. In: Proceedings of the 52nd Annual Meeting of the Association for Computational Linguistics (Volume 1: Long Papers), vol. 1, pp. 1155–1165 (2014)

Monitoring the Business Cycle with Fine-Grained, Aspect-Based Sentiment Extraction from News

Luca Barbaglia, Sergio Consoli$^{(\boxtimes)}$(iD), and Sebastiano Manzan

European Commission, Joint Research Centre, Directorate A-Strategy,
Work Programme and Resources, Scientific Development Unit,
Via E. Fermi 2749, 21027 Ispra, VA, Italy
{luca.barbaglia,sergio.consoli,sebastiano.manzan}@ec.europa.eu

Abstract. We provide an overview on the development of a fine-grained, aspect-based sentiment analysis approach aimed at providing useful signals to improve forecasts of economic models and produce more accurate predictions. The approach is unsupervised since it relies on external lexical resources to associate a polarity score to a given term or concept. After providing an overview of the method under development, some preliminary findings are also given.

Keywords: Economic forecasting and nowcasting · Semantic reasoning · Sentiment analysis · News analysis

1 Introduction

Governments, international organizations, and central banks rely heavily on economic forecasts to design economic and fiscal policies and their accuracy is particularly relevant during times of economic turmoil. Understanding, for example, the drivers of the recent downturn in Europe is of paramount importance for policy makers in order to learn how to avoid socially and economically stressful events as well as decide how to optimally react should these events happen again.

However, modern economies are subject to numerous shocks that make this task extremely difficult, both in the short and in the medium-long run. Therefore accuracy of economic forecasts is still problematic in a global interconnected economy where shocks move quickly through financial markets.

Furthermore, usual work in macroeconomic forecasting currently rely on official statistics that are released monthly or quarterly (or even longer), after the current month or quarter is ended. However central banks and governments need to know in real-time the state of economy, in particular during times of economic and financial distress.

To deal with these issues, economic forecasting and nowcasting can benefit from the availability of novel large data and by the rapid advances of data

---

Authors are listed in alphabetic order.

© Springer Nature Switzerland AG 2020
V. Bitetta et al. (Eds.): MIDAS 2019, LNAI 11985, pp. 101–106, 2020.
https://doi.org/10.1007/978-3-030-37720-5_8

analysis techniques, like those from machine learning and semantic reasoning, in order to produce more accurate and real-time indicators of economic activity.

In currently on-going research we are exploring whether economic news can be used to gauge the state of the business cycle. We believe that news are a promising nowcasting tool since they describe current economic events and the expectations of economic agents about the future. In particular understanding the sentiment embedded in the current economic news articles may provide information about the future state of the economy, yielding additional useful signals to improve forecasts of economic models and produce more accurate predictions [4].

Recent work in economics on the application of sentiment analysis from social media and news (e.g. [1,3,5,12]) generally suffers from: (i) a limited scope of historical financial news available; (ii) analysis of short texts only (e.g. usually tweets or news headlines); and (iii) use of basic, naïve in some cases, text analysis/natural language processing (NLP) techniques.

The goal of our analysis is to extract a sentiment signal from news articles that can be useful for forecasting economic indicators by: (i) considering longer time periods; (ii) analysing the entire text contained in the news articles; and (iii) using more sophisticated semantic reasoning techniques.

2   Literature Review

News articles represent a recent addition to the standard information used to model economic and financial variables. An early paper is [9] that uses sentiment from a column in the Wall Street Journal to show that high levels of pessimism are a relevant predictor of convergence of the stock prices towards their fundamental values. Following this early work, several other papers have tried to understand the role that news play in predicting, for instance, company news announcements, stock returns and volatility. Recently, news have been also used in macroeconomics. For example, [6] looks at the informational content of the Federal Reserve statements and the guidance that these statements provide about the future evolution of monetary policy. Other papers ([8,10,11] among others) use Latent Dirichlet allocation (LDA) to classify articles in topics and calculate simple measures of sentiment based on the topic classification. The goal of these papers is to extract a signal that could have some predictive content for measures of economic activity, such as GDP, unemployment and inflation. Their results show that economic sentiment is a useful addition to the toll-set of predictors that are commonly used to monitor and forecast the business cycle. A recent overview of the application of text mining to economics and finance is provided in [5].

3   Data

We used a dataset of economic news obtained from a commercial provider[1]. The dataset consisted of several million economic and financial articles, full-text, since 1994 (25 years exactly). We considered the following countries: United States, United Kingdom, Ireland, Spain, Italy, France, The Netherlands, Belgium, and Germany. For each country the largest and most popular domain outlets were selected. For example, for the United States we chose The New York Times, The Wall Street Journal, and The Washington Post. For the selected outlets, we considered only news belonging to the categories: Economic News (ECAT) and Commodity/Financial Market News (MCAT).

4   Fine-Grained, Aspect-Based Sentiment Analysis Approach

Sentiment analysis (SA) [7], also known as opinion mining, is a Semantic Web technology directly related to Natural Language Processing [2]. It aims at understanding whether a certain message conveys a positive or negative sentiment with respect to a certain topic, or the overall contextual polarity or emotional reaction to a document, interaction, or event. Attitude might be a quantitative/qualitative polarity (e.g. $[-1 : -1]$, *extr neg, neg, neut, pos, extr pos*, etc.) or an emotional state (e.g. *joy, anger*, etc.).

In particular, in our work we use a fine-grained, aspect-based sentiment analysis approach [7]. With "aspect-based" we intend that our SA approach is able to recognize the entity to which the sentiment aspect is expressed, while with "fine-grained" means that the detected sentiment polarity is given by means of a continuous value in a certain range (e.g. $[-1, +1]$). In addition, our approach is an unsupervised one, which relies on external lexical resources or specific dictionaries to come up with a polarity score for a given term or concept.

The method works as follow. Suppose we want to extract from our news data the sentiment polarity referred to a specific economic concept, e.g. *industrial production*. First, its economic synonyms are derived by means of SPARQL queries against the *World Bank Group Ontology*[2]. For example, for *industrial production*, the economic synonyms are obtained: *manufacturing*; *industrial output*; *secondary sector*; *industry productivity*; *manufacturing development*; *industrial growth*; *manufacturing productivity*; etc.

Then a NLP pipeline is used. First, by using a rule-based Information Extraction (IE) procedure, based on the linguistic features of the *spaCy* Python library[3], structured information [2] that relates to our search concepts are

---

[1] Dow Jones DNA: Data, News and Analytics Platform: https://www.dowjones.com/dna/.

[2] World Bank Group Ontology, available at: http://vocabulary.worldbank.org/thesaurus.html.

[3] spaCy: Industrial-Strength Natural Language Processing. Available at: https://spacy.io/.

extracted from the news data. This NLP pipeline relies on the *en_core_web_lg* model of spaCy[4], an English multi-task Convolutional Neural Network trained on OntoNotes, with GloVe vectors trained on Common Crawl, which assigns word vectors, context-specific token vectors, Part-of-speech (POS) tags, dependency parse and named entities. The following NLP steps are performed [2]:

- *Tokenization & lemmatization*: News text is split into meaningful segments (*tokens*), considering uninflected form of the words (*lemmas*) in the text taken from WordNet[5].
- *Named Entity Recognition*: Named-entity mentions in the news text are located and classified, including locations, organizations, time expressions, quantities, monetary values, etc.
- *Most frequent location heuristic*: Heuristic brocedure which assigns the location to which a sentence is referring, as its most frequent named-entity location detected in the sentence text.
- *POS tagging*: News text is parsed and tagged using spaCy's stastical model. We loop over the POS tree stopping when our search concept, or one of its synomyms, is found.
- *Dependency Parsing*: After our search concept is found, we navigate over the neighbouring tokens employing a rule-based approach leveraging on syntactic dependency parsing. Chunks of terms related to our search concepts are constructed.
- *Tense detection heuristic*: Heuristic procedure used to detect the tense of the constructed terms chunks extracted from the news and related to our search concept through our rule-based approach.
- *Negation handling*: Whenever a negation term is detected in a terms chuck, the related derived sentiment score is inverted.

At this step, after the employed NLP pipeline constructs a concatenated chunks of terms related to our search concepts, the sentiment polarity of each term is taken from a custom economics vocabulary we are building, or from Senti-WordNet[6], a lexical resource in which each WordNet synset is associatcd to three numerical scores, describing respectively how objective, positive, and negative the terms contained in the synset are. Positivity or negativity of the obtained polarity score is double-checked against the Loughran-McDonald dictionary[7], a thesaurus of economic terms categorized as Negative, Positive, Uncertainty, Litigious, Strong Modal, Weak Modal, Constraining). Finally, sentiment scores of the terms contained in a chunk are properly propagated to the root search concept, providing a final polarity score for it.

---

[4] https://spacy.io/models/en.
[5] WordNet, A Lexical Database for English. Available at https://wordnet.princeton.edu/.
[6] SentiWordNet, available at http://swn.isti.cnr.it/.
[7] Loughran-McDonald Sentiment Word Lists, available at: https://sraf.nd.edu/textual-analysis/resources/.

5   Preliminary Findings and Conclusions

We construct daily sentiment indicators using the methodology described in the previous section on four topics that represent broad categories of economic variables:

- *Output*: news that relate to industrial production, services, manufacturing and other keywords related to the quantity side of the economy
- *Prices*: in this category we look at text that relates to producer and consumer prices, inflation, and commodity prices among others
- *Labour*: news that relates to the job market, unemployment, and lay-offs
- *Monetary*: topics related to the monetary and finance situation, such as interest rates, term structure, and bond markets in general.

The first part of our analysis tries to understand the relationship between the news flow and the release of macroeconomic variables by the statistical agencies. We focus in particular on the United States for which release dates are available on a wide range of variables. We find that a large portion of the news are produced the days before and after the news release. However, there are significant spillover effects from announcements about a variable on other macroeconomic variables which can potentially be useful for forecasting. The second goal of the paper is to use aspect-based sentiment indicators to predict measures of economic activity. We are particularly interested in nowcasting the economic variables, that is, forecast the value of a variable during month t when the official release of the value will occur only at the mid of month $t + 1$. For the US the delay in the release ranges from a few days for labor variables to two weeks for production variables, to about 3 weeks for national accounts variables. For Europe the typical delay in release ranges from 30 to 45 days. The goal of the analysis is thus to nowcast the value of the economic variable in real-time and before the official release of the statistical agencies. We use standard forecasting models augmented by the four news indicators described above and compare their performance relative to the models without news. The results show that news are particularly useful in nowcasting European variables, which is particularly useful due to the long delay in the release. In addition, we find that output and inflation sentiment are relevant predictors also for labour and monetary variables. Overall, our analysis provides evidence of the usefulness of considering news as a additional instrument in the nowcasting tool-set of macroeconomists.

References

1. Agrawal, S., Azar, P., Lo, A.W., Singh, T.: Momentum, mean-reversion and social media: evidence from StockTwits and Twitter. J. Portf. Manag. **44**, 85–95 (2018)
2. Consoli, S., Recupero, D.R.: Using FRED for named entity resolution, linking and typing for knowledge base population. Commun. Comput. Inform. Sci. **548**, 40–50 (2015)

3. Dridi, A., Atzeni, M., Recupero, D.R.: FineNews: fine-grained semantic sentiment analysis on financial microblogs and news. Int. J. Mach. Learn. Cybern. **10**(8), 2199–2207 (2019)
4. Fabbi, C., Righi, A., Testa, P., Valentino, L., Zardetto, D.: Social mood on economy index. In: XIII Conferenza Nazionale di Statistica (2018)
5. Gentzkow, M., Kelly, B., Taddy, M.: Text as data. J. Econ. Lit. (2019, to appear)
6. Hansen, S., McMahon, M.: Shocking language: understanding the macroeconomic effects of central bank communication. J. Int. Econ. **99**, S114–S133 (2016)
7. Recupero, D.R., Presutti, V., Consoli, S., Gangemi, A., Nuzzolese, A.G.: Sentilo: frame-based sentiment analysis. Cogn. Comput. **7**, 211–225 (2015)
8. Shapiro, A.H., Sudhof, M., Wilson, D.: Measuring news sentiment. Federal Reserve Bank of San Francisco Working Paper (2018)
9. Tetlock, P.C.: Giving content to investor sentiment: the role of media in the stock market. J. Financ. **62**(3), 1139–1168 (2007)
10. Thorsrud, L.A.: Nowcasting using news topics. big data versus big bank. Norges Bank Working Paper (2016)
11. Thorsrud, L.A.: Words are the new numbers: a newsy coincident index of the business cycle. J. Bus. Econ. Stat. 1–17 (2018, in press)
12. Tuckett, D.: Conviction narrative theory and understanding decision-making in economics and finance. In: Uncertain Futures: Imaginaries, Narratives, and Calculation in the Economy, pp. 62–82 (2018)

Multi-step Prediction of Financial Asset Return Volatility Using Parsimonious Autoregressive Sequential Model

Xiangru Fan[1]([⊠])(iD), Xiaoqian Wei[2], Di Wang[1], Wen Zhang[1], and Wu Qi[3]

[1] JD.com, Beijing 102600, China
fanxiangru@jd.com, albertwang0921@gmail.com, zhangwen.jd@gmail.com
[2] Peiking University, Beijing 100000, China
weixiaoqian@pku.edu.cn
[3] City University of Hongkong, Hongkong, SAR, China
qiwu55@cityu.edu.hk

Abstract. Previously, application of deep learning based sequential model drastically improved accuracy of volatility prediction in modelling of financial time series. However, unlike traditional financial time series model such as GARCH family of models, majority of deep learning based financial time series models focus solely on optimizing a single-step volatility prediction error and are not capable of conduct multi-step training and prediction of volatilities since volatility is the inherent uncertainty of the model prediction, whose multi-step prediction is drastically different from prediction of the mean of the financial time series.

In this work, a parsimonious autoregressive multi-step density regression (PA-MS-DR) framework is proposed to solve this problem. Our model framework can accurately capture the heavy-tail property of financial asset returns. In addition, our model is autoregressive, and it allows multi-step ahead training and forecasting, which significantly expands the applicability of the model in real world scenario. Finally, the structure of our method inspires us to devise a novel training method, which greatly accelerates the training speed of the algorithm.

The performance of PA-MS-DR is tested by comparing it with traditional time series models such as GARCH family of models and a non-autoregressive baseline model with similar structure. The result shows that our model consistently and significantly outperforms GARCH family of models. In addition, our model consistently outperforms the non-autoregressive baseline model, which demonstrates the effectiveness of our autoregressive model structure.

Keywords: Financial time series · Multi-step volatility prediction · Nested gated recurrent unit

1 Introduction

For modelling financial time-series, multi-step prediction is often preferred over single-step prediction. Model that conducts multi-step prediction takes the

© Springer Nature Switzerland AG 2020
V. Bitetta et al. (Eds.): MIDAS 2019, LNAI 11985, pp. 107–121, 2020.
https://doi.org/10.1007/978-3-030-37720-5_9

historical values of a time sequence as input and outputs the predicted values at multiple future time-steps instead of single future time-step [20]. As an example, stock market investors leaned on long-term anticipation of financial asset market performance to determine their trading strategy, which requires accurate prediction of asset returns in the next few days. Despite its importance, multi-step prediction model requires specialized model structure and training strategy [20] that make them less popular than single-step models.

Comparing with most other multi-step prediction problems, such as word-by-word sentence prediction and machine translation, multi-step prediction of financial time series is significantly harder. This is because while most other multi-step prediction tasks focus on prediction of the mean value of the prediction target, the financial time series prediction task focuses on prediction of the variance of the target (volatility in terms of financial engineering), since the mean value prediction in most financial asset return time-series, such as stock index and foreign exchange rates, is pointless due to the highly stochastic nature of financial market. Therefore, in this paper, we proposed a novel deep-learning based approach that enables multi-step volatility prediction.

A naïve approach for solving multi-step prediction problem is simply to treat each future-step as a separate prediction target, i.e.

$$pdt_{L+1} = model1(obs_1, obs_2, ..., obs_L))$$
$$pdt_{L+2} = model2(obs_1, obs_2, ..., obs_L))$$
$$...$$
$$pdt_{L+H} = model2(obs_1, obs_2, ..., obs_L))$$

where obs_L means observation at time L, and pdt_{L+1} means prediction at time L+1. As can be seen in literature, this method is widely applied when precise modelling of multi-step ahead dynamics is not important. However, this method is suboptimal since it completely ignored the interdependency between future time steps. Another less obvious approach to solve the multi-step ahead prediction problem would be the recursive method, which uses the prediction result of previous time-step to predict current time step until all future time-steps are recursively predicted.

$$pdt_{L+1} = model(obs_1, obs_2, ..., obs_L))$$
$$pdt_{L+2} = model(obs_1, ..., obs_L, pdt_{L+1})$$
$$...$$
$$pdt_{L+H} = model(obs_1, ..., pdt_{L+H-2}, pdt_{L+H-1})$$

This method is widely applied in traditional time-series modelling methods such as GARCH family of models. Nevertheless, this method requires the underlying model used to be an autoregressive model, which is not satisfied for majority of deep learning based models.

A previous study by Yan et al. [21] demonstrated the superior performance of deep-learning based model over traditional autoregressive methods, such as

GARCH, at predicting the conditional probability distribution of asset returns. In their work, they use long short-term memory (LSTM) sequential model to extract feature from past asset return series and predict current conditional quantile of the asset return. In addition to its high precision, their method can capture the heavy-tail property of financial asset returns, which is crucial for application of the model in real world financial market. However, with sophisticated design of features and aiming at predict conditional quantile rather than probability density function (PDF), their model is no longer autoregressive and cannot be applied to conduct recursive multi-step prediction. In addition, quantile regression models are less interpretable than probabilistic regression models, whose statistical properties, such as mean, variance and skewness are well-established.

In this paper, we propose an autoregressive distribution regression framework called parsimonious autoregressive multi-step density regression (PA-MS-DR) that conduct recursive multi-step prediction of probability density function and can tackle the heavy-tail problem of financial time series. The PA-MS-DR framework uses gated recurrent unit (GRU) [5] to extract information from past time-steps and predict the distribution parameters of the PDF. The predicted PDF of current time-step is converted into input of next time-step, and recursively feed to the model again to produce the prediction of next time-step. This autoregressive structure involves no additional parameters, thus is parsimonious, yet it can outperform more heavily parametrized baseline models. The PA-MS-DR model supports regression of multiple types of probability density function, notably the normal distribution and t-distribution, which can be used to model heavy-tailed financial asset return distributions. The model structure of PA-MS-DR contains a nested RNN substructure, which slows down training of the model, to accelerate the training process, we invent a novel approximate back-propagation-through-time algorithm specifically for PA-MS-DR model and its convergence is mathematically proved.

Specifically, we make the following contributions in this paper:

- We proposed an efficient GRU based density regression model (PA-MS-DR) that significantly outperformed traditional GARCH family of models on prediction of financial asset return distribution.
- The PA-MS-DR model we proposed contains a parameter free autoregressive structure and can be exploited to conduct recurrent multi-step ahead prediction.
- A highly efficient training algorithm for the PA-MS-DR model is proposed and its convergence is theoretically proved.

The rest of the paper is organized as follows. In Sect. 2, we introduce GARCH family of models, which is closely related to our models. In Sect. 3, the detailed structure of the model is discussed step by step. Then, in Sect. 4, the experiment conditions and the performance comparison of the model with baseline models are given. We conclude our work in Sect. 5.

2 Recursive Multi-step Prediction Using GARCH Family of Models

The generalized autoregressive conditional heteroskedasicity (GARCH) family of models are used extensively in the field of financial engineering to predict the conditional distribution of financial asset returns given past performance of the financial asset [2]. Using GARCH (p, q) as an example, the model can be summarized in the following equations:

$$r_t = u_t + \epsilon_t, \quad \epsilon_t \sim N(0, \sigma^2) \tag{1}$$

$$\sigma_t^2 = \omega + \alpha_1 \epsilon_{t-1}^2 + \ldots + \alpha_p \epsilon_{t-1}^2 + \beta_1 \sigma_{t-1}^2 + \ldots + \beta_q \sigma_{t-1}^2 \tag{2}$$

where r_t is the asset return to be modelled, u_t is the mean of the asset return at time t, ϵ_t is the residual, which follows a normal distribution N with variance σ^2. Parameters ω, α_1 to α_p and β_1 to β_q are model parameters to be estimated.

There are several variants of GARCH. The original version of GARCH model [2] assumes that the residual follows normal distribution $\epsilon_t \sim N(0, \sigma^2)$, but this is inaccurate in reflecting the real-life financial asset return, which is often heavy-tail distributed. An alternative version of GARCH model assumes that the residual follows t-distribution, i.e. $\epsilon_t \sim t(df, 0, \sigma^2)$, where df is the degree of freedom. This method is named GARCH-t. Several variants of GARCH method attempt to modify Eq. (2), such as GJR-GARCH [13], which introduces an asymmetric innovation term into Eq. (2). Both the original version of GARCH, GJR-GARCH and their corresponding t-distribution variant are considered in this study.

The conditional mean term u_t in GARCH model can be modelled separately by other models. Frequently, it can be regarded as a constant $u_t = u$, or modelled by linear autoregressive formula $u_t = \gamma_0 + \gamma_1 r_{t-1} + \ldots + \gamma_n r_{t-2}$. GARCH model with this linear autoregressive conditional mean is denoted as AR-GARCH, AR-GARCH-t, etc.

Since GARCH family of models are autoregressive, it can be easily extended to conduct multi-step ahead predictions.

For $h = 1$ (single step forecasting)

$$\sigma_{t+1}^2 = \omega + \alpha \epsilon_t^2 + \beta \sigma_t^2 \quad \text{if} \quad h = 1 \tag{3}$$

$$\sigma_{t+1+h}^2 = \omega + \alpha E[\epsilon_{t+h}^2] + \beta \sigma_{t+h}^2 \quad \text{if} \quad h \geq 1 \tag{4}$$

The above equation can be simplified to $\sigma_{t+1+h}^2 = \omega + (\alpha + \beta)\sigma_{t+h}^2$ by exploiting the fact that ϵ_{t+h} follows normal distribution with mean 0 and variance σ_{t+h}, hence $E[\epsilon_{t+h}^2] = \sigma_{t+h}^2$

Besides GARCH, the stochastic volatility (SV) type of models are also applicable to recursively predict multi-step ahead conditional distribution of asset return. Nevertheless, their underlying assumption is essentially different from the GARCH model, which focuses solely on the serial dependency of conditional volatilities and is more suitable to be compared directly with our GRU-based neural network models. Extensive comparison of SV model and GARCH model is made in [4,11,12,19]. Several other recently proposed models, such as [10,21], while also focus on sequence prediction, are nevertheless focusing on quantile regression rather then prediction of PDF. Hence, the GARCH type recursive multi-step ahead prediction strategy are not suitable for them, which makes direct comparison with them infeasible.

3   The Model

In this section, we introduce our model one step a time. We first briefly introduce methods for modelling conditional probability density function (conditional density estimation), then we demonstrate how conditional density estimation combined with temporal sequence modelling can be used to estimate probability distribution of financial asset return. Finally, we introduce our multi-step ahead autoregressive model together with its training method.

3.1   Conditional Density Estimation

Conditional density estimation method aims at prediction of the conditional probability distribution $p(y|x)$ of variable y given feature vector x[8]. Several broad category of methods can be used to accomplish this task, including Bayesian density regression [18], which assumes the conditional density to be a mixture of certain prior distributions, and probabilistic regression models (density regression), which assumes that the dependent variable y follows certain known family of distributions. Both GARCH methods and methods proposed in this paper belong to the latter category.

For simplicity, we uses GARCH(1, 1) model (Eqs. (1) and (2), with p and q equal to 1) as the example to demonstrate the general process of probabilistic regression models. Given a dataset $\{x_i, y_i\}_{i=1}^{N}$, fitting a GARCH(1, 1) model on the dataset is to finding the optimum parameters ω, α_1 and β_1 that maximize the log-likelihood of the model.

The log-likelihood $log(\mathcal{L})$ is as follows:

$$log(\mathcal{L}(y|x; \omega, \alpha_1, \beta_1) = log(\prod_{n=1}^{N} p(y_n|x_n; \omega, \alpha_1, \beta_1) \tag{5}$$

$$= \sum_{n=1}^{N} log(p(y_n|x_n; \omega, \alpha_1, \beta_1) \tag{6}$$

$$= \sum_{n=1}^{N} log(\frac{1}{\sqrt{2\pi}\sigma_n} e^{\frac{-(y_n - \mu_n)^2}{2\sigma_n^2}}) \tag{7}$$

$$= \sum_{n=1}^{N} \frac{-(y_n - \mu_n)^2}{2\sigma_n^2} + log(\frac{1}{\sqrt{2\pi}\sigma_n}) \tag{8}$$

where $\sigma_t^2 = \omega + \alpha_1 \epsilon_{t-1}^2 + \beta_1 \sigma_{t-1}^2$, t is the time step number. ϵ_{t-1}, σ_{t-1} comes from previous time-steps, which is treated as feature vector x_n. μ is the mean, which is usually set to be a constant. It should be noted that Eq. (6) assumes the underlying distribution of the asset returns to follow a normal distribution, which is valid only in vanilla GARCH model and is not applicable to the GARCH-t as well as the t-distribution version of our proposed model. The optimum value of parameters ω, α_1 and β_1 can be estimated by minimizing the negative of Eq. (8) using gradient descent method or other gradient free optimization methods. Similar to the GARCH method discussed above, our proposed method (normal distribution variant) is also trained by minimizing the negative log-likelihood (Eq. (8)), except that the σ is parametrized by a GRU based sequential model. The t-distribution version of our proposed model substitutes Eq. (7) with following equation: $\sum_{n=1}^{N} log(\frac{\Gamma(\frac{df+1}{2})}{\sqrt{df\pi\sigma^2}\Gamma(\frac{df}{2})}(\frac{1}{df}(\frac{x-\mu}{\sigma})^2+1)^{-\frac{df+1}{2}})$, terms inside the log sign is the PDF of the t-distribution, the additional parameter df is the degree of freedom, which is treated as a pre-determined constant in this study.

3.2 Single-Step Density Regression Using Gated Recurrent Unit Model

Our first move is to enrich the expressiveness of density regression with GRU based temporal sequence models and construct a set of features that is suitable to apply GRU on it.

To facilitate discussion of the model, we use a 3-step ahead normal distribution regression $\mathcal{N}(\mu, \sigma^2)$ as an example, where μ is the mean and σ is the standard deviation of the normal distribution. Nevertheless, it is note worthy that the model prediction time-horizon can be any positive integral and the model is designed to be applicable to a wide spectrum of families of distribution, including the t-distribution, which play a critical role in modelling financial asset return.

Similar to GARCH family of models, the distribution parameters μ and σ are assumed to be conditional on past financial return series $r_{t-1}, r_{t-2}, \dots$. However, the GARCH family of models all assume that the distribution variance is a linear function of computed conditional variances and observed value of previous time step, which may be insufficient to describe the complex dynamics of financial time series. To model that, we chose the gated recurrent unit (GRU) based sequential model and applied it on a $L \times 4$ shaped raw feature matrix that incorporate the first, second, third and fourth power of observed value r. In detail, the raw feature matrix is as follows:

$$x_1, x_2, \dots, x_L = \begin{bmatrix} r_1 \\ r_1^2 \\ r_1^3 \\ r_1^4 \end{bmatrix}, \begin{bmatrix} r_2 \\ r_2^2 \\ r_2^3 \\ r_2^4 \end{bmatrix}, \dots, \begin{bmatrix} r_L \\ r_L^2 \\ r_L^3 \\ r_L^4 \end{bmatrix}$$

The intuition behind this choice of features is because the expected value of them, $E(r)$, $E(r^2)$, $E(r^3)$ and $E(r^4)$ is the first, second, third and fourth order raw momentum and they are closely related to the mean, variance, skewness and kurtosis of the distribution.

The hidden state outputted by GRU is then used as feature to regress the distribution parameters:

$$h = \mathbf{GRU}(x_1, x_2, ..., x_L; \Theta) \tag{9}$$

$$[\mu_{L+1}, \sigma_{L+1}]^T = \phi(W_1 h + b_1) \tag{10}$$

where Θ is the parameters used inside GRU model, W_1 and b_1 are the output layer parameters. ϕ is a non-linear activation function, which is set to be a modified version of rectified linear units that took the form $\phi(x) = min(x, 0.1)$. Training of the model involves minimizing the negative of log-likelihood $log(\mathcal{L})$ (Eq. (8)) with respect to the model parameters. i.e.

$$\underset{\Theta, W_1, b_1}{\arg\min} - \sum_{n=1}^{N} \frac{-(y_n - \mu_n)^2}{2\sigma_n^2} + log(\frac{1}{\sqrt{2\pi}\sigma_n}) \tag{11}$$

Combines Eqs. (9–11) completes the single-step version of our model. This model is named single-step density regression (SS-DR), which serves as the starting point for our proposed method.

To allow multi-step prediction, a naive approach will be adding multiply output to Eq. (10):

$$h = \mathbf{GRU}(x_1, x_2, ..., x_L; \Theta) \tag{12}$$

$$[\mu_{L+1}, \sigma_{L+1}]^T = \phi(W_1 h + b_1) \tag{13}$$

$$[\mu_{L+2}, \sigma_{L+2}]^T = \phi(W_2 h + b_2) \tag{14}$$

$$[\mu_{L+3}, \sigma_{L+3}]^T = \phi(W_3 h + b_3) \tag{15}$$

The training process for this multiple-step prediction then becomes finding model parameters $\Theta, W_1, b_1, W_2, b_2, W_3, b_3$ that maximize the log-likelihood $log(\mathcal{L})$.

$$\underset{\Theta, W_1, b_1, ..., W_3, b_3}{\arg\max} \sum_{n=1}^{N} \sum_{l=1}^{3} log(p(y_n | x_n; \Theta, W_l, b_l)) \tag{16}$$

This model is named multi-step density regression (MS-DR), which serves as a baseline model in this study.

3.3   Parsimonious Autoregressive Multi-step Density Regression (PA-MS-DR)

Our second move introduces recursive multi-step prediction to the SS-DR model by adding a differentiable feature processing layer that convert PDF prediction of current time-step into model input of next time-step (thus makes the model an autoregressive model) and then recursively predict PDFs of all future steps.

One major difficulty lies in that the SS-DR model predict the mean μ and variance σ^2 of the PDF $\mathcal{N}(\mu, \sigma^2)$ that r follows instead of directly predict r. A method to convert PDF into model input of next time-step is required in order to create an autoregressive model.

One approach to solve this problem is by using the expected value of r, r^2, r^3 and r^4 as model input. Consider randomly drawn N number of random values r_n from the predicted PDF $\mathcal{N}(\mu, \sigma^2)$, as N approaches inf, its average value $\sum_{n=1}^{N} r_n$ will approach the expected value $E(r)$. This is also the method used by the GARCH model.

The definition of $E(r)$, $E(r^2)$, $E(r^3)$ and $E(r^4)$ coincide with the definition of first, second, third and fourth order raw momentum and they can be computed as follows:

$$E(r) = f_{E(r)}(\mu, \sigma) = \int_{-\infty}^{\infty} r \frac{1}{\sqrt{2\pi}\sigma} e^{\frac{-(r-\mu)^2}{2\sigma^2}} d(r) \tag{17}$$

$$E(r^2) = f_{E(r^2)}(\mu, \sigma) = \int_{-\infty}^{\infty} r^2 \frac{1}{\sqrt{2\pi}\sigma} e^{\frac{-(r-\mu)^2}{2\sigma^2}} d(r) \tag{18}$$

$$E(r^3) = f_{E(r^3)}(\mu, \sigma) = \int_{-\infty}^{\infty} r^3 \frac{1}{\sqrt{2\pi}\sigma} e^{\frac{-(r-\mu)^2}{2\sigma^2}} d(r) \tag{19}$$

$$E(r^4) = f_{E(r^4)}(\mu, \sigma) = \int_{-\infty}^{\infty} r^4 \frac{1}{\sqrt{2\pi}\sigma} e^{\frac{-(r-\mu)^2}{2\sigma^2}} d(r) \tag{20}$$

For a normal distribution, the analytical solution for above equations is known:

$$E(r) = \mu \tag{21}$$
$$E(r^2) = \mu^2 + \sigma^2 \tag{22}$$
$$E(r^3) = \mu^3 + 3\mu\sigma^2 \tag{23}$$
$$E(r^4) = \mu^4 + 6\mu^2\sigma^2 + 3\sigma^4 \tag{24}$$

However, for distributions other then normal distribution, the analytical expression of $E(r)$, $E(r^2)$, $E(r^3)$ and $E(r^4)$ become overwhelmingly complex, some of them even does not have known analytical form. t-distribution is a common example.

The integration term causes difficulty in construction of the model. Previous study by Mei et al. [17] uses Monte-Carlo estimation to handle the integration term inside their model. Besides, in certain variants of GARCH model, Monte-Carlo estimation are also used. However, Monte-Carlo estimation introduces stochasticity into the training process hence dramatically slows down training. To solve this problem, we introduce the Gauss-Legendre quadrature rule from the field of numerical analysis to conduct accurate numerical integration [14]. The Gauss-Legendre integration quadrature rule approximate integration equation in Eq. (17) with a summation, as follows:

$$E(r) = \int_{-\infty}^{\infty} r \frac{1}{\sqrt{2\pi}\sigma} e^{\frac{-(r-\mu)^2}{2\sigma^2}} d(r) \tag{25}$$

$$\approx \sum_{i=1}^{n} w_i r_i \frac{1}{\sqrt{2\pi}\sigma} e^{\frac{-(r_i-\mu)^2}{2\sigma^2}} \tag{26}$$

Where sample locations r_i and sample weights w_i are computed by the Gauss-Legendre integration quadrature rule. A brief introduction of the Gauss-Legendre quadrature rule and test of precision of this integration schema is given in appendix A in supplementary material[1].

Using this method, the $E(r)$, $E(r^2)$, $E(r^3)$ and $E(r^4)$ can be computed and then, x_{t+1} will be known. We can feed the predicted x_{t+1} back into the model, and conduct recursive multi-step prediction. Equations (27–31) summarize the overall prediction procedure of PA-MS-DR model.

$$[\mu_{L+1}, \sigma_{L+1}]^T = \phi(\boldsymbol{W}\mathbf{GRU}(\boldsymbol{x}_1, \boldsymbol{x}_2, ..., \boldsymbol{x}_L) + \boldsymbol{b}) \tag{27}$$

$$x_{L+1} = \begin{bmatrix} f_{E(r)}([\mu_{L+1}, \sigma_{L+1}]^T) \\ f_{E(r^2)}([\mu_{L+1}, \sigma_{L+1}]^T) \\ f_{E(r^3)}([\mu_{L+1}, \sigma_{L+1}]^T) \\ f_{E(r^4)}([\mu_{L+1}, \sigma_{L+1}]^T) \end{bmatrix} \tag{28}$$

$$[\mu_{L+2}, \sigma_{L+2}]^T = \phi(\boldsymbol{W}\mathbf{GRU}(\boldsymbol{x}_1, \boldsymbol{x}_2, ..., \boldsymbol{x}_{L+1}) + \boldsymbol{b}) \tag{29}$$

$$x_{L+2} = \begin{bmatrix} f_{E(r)}([\mu_{L+2}, \sigma_{L+2}]^T) \\ f_{E(r^2)}([\mu_{L+2}, \sigma_{L+2}]^T) \\ f_{E(r^3)}([\mu_{L+2}, \sigma_{L+2}]^T) \\ f_{E(r^4)}([\mu_{L+2}, \sigma_{L+2}]^T) \end{bmatrix} \tag{30}$$

$$[\mu_{L+3}, \sigma_{L+3}]^T = \phi(\boldsymbol{W}\mathbf{GRU}(\boldsymbol{x}_1, \boldsymbol{x}_2, ..., \boldsymbol{x}_{L+2}) + \boldsymbol{b}) \tag{31}$$

---

[1] Supplementary material is available at https://github.com/imo1991/appendix4 papers.

Algorithm 1. Segregated BPTT training of PA-MS-DR

1: **procedure** TRAINING
2:    $x_{L+1}^0, x_{L+2}^0, x_{L+3}^0 = 0, 0, 0$
3:    $g_{L+1}^0, g_{L+2}^0, g_{L+3}^0 = 0, 0, 0$
4:    $k = 1$
5:    **for** $k <= TrainSteps$ **do**
6:        compute $[\mu_{L+1}^k, \sigma_{L+1}^k]^T$ from $x_0, ..., x_L$ using Eq. (27)
7:        compute $[\mu_{L+2}^k, \sigma_{L+2}^k]^T$ from $x_0, ..., x_L$ and x_{L+1}^{k-1} using Eq. (29)
8:        compute $[\mu_{L+3}^k, \sigma_{L+3}^k]^T$ from $x_0, ..., x_L$ as well as $x_{L+1}^{k-1}, x_{L+2}^{k-1}$ using Eq. (31)
9:        compute x_{L+1}^k from $[\mu_{L+1}^k, \sigma_{L+1}^k]^T$ using Eq. (28)
10:       compute x_{L+2}^k from $[\mu_{L+2}^k, \sigma_{L+2}^k]^T$ using Eq. (30)
11:
12:       $g_{L+1}^k = \frac{\partial MLEloss_{L+1}}{\partial x_{L+1}} + g_{L+2}^{k-1} \frac{\partial x_{L+2}^k}{\partial x_{L+1}^k}$
13:       $g_{L+2}^k = \frac{\partial MLEloss_{L+2}}{\partial x_{L+2}} + g_{L+2}^{k-1} \frac{\partial x_{L+3}^k}{\partial x_{L+2}^k}$
14:       $g_{L+3}^k = \frac{\partial MLEloss_{L+3}}{\partial x_{L+3}}$
15:       back-propagation use $g_{L+1}^k, g_{L+2}^k, g_{L+3}^k$ and update parameters
16:    **end for**
17: **end procedure**

3.4   Training of the PA-MS-DR Model

As shown in Eqs. (27–31), the final model PA-MS-DR wrapped a whole GRU model inside a recurrent neural network (RNN) struture, thus constitute a nested RNN, which slows down training. Although traditional back propagation through time (BPTT) method can be applied to train this model, its performance is nevertheless unsatisfactory due to excessively long temporal dependency between time steps in this model [1,3,16].

This problem of accelerating the training of RNN to be as fast as convolutional neural networks (CNN) has attracted the attention of many researchers. In Lei's work [16], the author proposed a highly efficient recurrent structured named simple recurrent unit (SRU), which accelerates the training by minimizing the temporal dependency between time steps. Inside the structure of SRU, all gates that controls information passing can be computed independent of time, the only temporal dependent component is the cell variable.

To accelerate training of the PA-MS-DR, we propose a novel training algorithm named segregated back-propagation-through-time methods (segregated BPTT, Algorithm 1) by exploiting the structure of the PA-MS-DR. Contrast with the SRU, our methods accelerate the training of RNN by modifying the training method instead of the recurrent structure. By using hidden states and gradients of hidden states from last gradient descent step, time steps of the RNN are decoupled, and parallelization in temporal dimension is now feasible. The detailed mathematical process involved is shown in Algorithm 1, x_{L+1}^0 is predicted feature x at future time-step 1 and optimization iteration 0. g_{L+1}^0 is gradient on x_{L+1}^0.

Our algorithm exploited the fact that in our model, information passed between consecutive time steps is relatively insignificant in comparison with conventional RNN. Our algorithm differs from normal BPTT algorithm in that instead of using hidden states passed from previous time step in current optimization iteration, hidden states from previous optimization iteration are used. Similarly, the gradients on the hidden states from previous optimization iteration are used instead of gradients from current optimization iteration. In this pattern, temporal dependency between consecutive prediction is truncated, and training of the network can be parallelized, hence greatly accelerating the training of the algorithm. Mathematical proof of the convergence of segregated BPTT training algorithm is given in appendix B in supplementary material, and experimental testing of the convergence and training speed of this algorithm on a broad range of recurrent neural networks is shown in appendix C.

4   Experiments

In this section, financial asset returns from real-world market, including major stock market indexes S&P 500, NASDAQ 100 and Nikkei 225, as well as major foreign exchange rates EUR-USD and JPY-USD, are selected to test the validity of our proposed method. The stock market datasets are daily asset returns from January 1995 to February 2019. The foreign exchange rate datasets are daily asset returns from January 1999 to February 2019. The asset return series is calculated by following formula: $r_t = P_t/P_{t-1} - 1$, where P_t is the closing price or rate at day t. Each time series is split along the time-line into three parts, namely training set, validation set and testing set. The training set contains the first nine tens of the original time series, and the validation set and testing set each contains one twentieth of the original time series.

For the PA-MS-DR model, the model parameters used are chosen by searching on S&P 500 dataset among lengths L= {20, 40, 60} and hidden unit numbers {1, 4, 8, 16}. Since the GRU layer is immediately connected with the output layer, the hidden unit numbers of the GRU layer is the only hyperparameter involved in this model. The output layer uses tanh activation function for mean value μ prediction and uses a customarily modified RELU activation function (RELU with lower bounds 0.1 instead of 0) for volatility σ prediction. For the GARCH family of models, which severs as baselines in this study, the lag order of symmetric innovation p, and lagged volatility q are all set to be the same as the sequence length used in our PA-MS-DR model. The degree of freedom parameter of t-distribution is determined by searching on S&P 500 dataset and EUR-USD dataset among $df = \{3, 6, 9, 12, 15\}$ using a two feature variant of our model, and df value that can produce model with highest negative log-likelihood is then selected. df selected is 9 for stock market indexes data and 15 for foreign exchange rate data. Eight variants of GARCH model and our non-autoregressive multi-step density regression model (MS-DR) are treated as baselines.

Table 1. The negative log-likelihood of on the train set of stock index S&P 500 and exchange rate EUR-USD. The multi-step forecasts of next 5 days are listed separately as H1, H2, H3, H4 and H5. The PA-MS-DR-t and MS-DR-t assumes t-distribution of stock returns. The degree of freedom of the t-distribution is set at 9. The PA-MS-DR and MS-DR assumes normal distribution.

(S&P 500) Future day	H1	H2	H3	H4	H5
PA-MS-DR-t	1.31351	1.3182	1.32308	1.32783	1.33416
MS-DR-t	1.32788	1.32985	1.33302	1.33541	1.34282
(EUR-USD)Future day	H1	H2	H3	H4	H5
PA-MS-DR	0.819344	0.822294	0.826547	0.828847	0.833771
MS-DR	0.834209	0.836135	0.838145	0.839928	0.845113

Model Fitting Ability. To compare our method (PA-MS-DR) with the non-autoregressive baseline method (MS-DR) in model fitting ability, we over-fit both models on the training set of S&P 500 and EUR-USD data. The negative log-likelihood results for prediction of all 5 future days are shown in Table 1. As it indicates, our method consistently outperformed the baseline methods in all future day predictions. Besides, our methods uses only two thirds of model parameters of baseline methods.

Testing of the Result on Real-World Market. We tested the trained models on real-world market data consisting of S&P500, NASDAQ 100, Nikkei 225, EUR-USD and JPY-USD. The negative log-likelihood results for prediction of all 5 assets are shown in Table 2. Under the t-distribution assumption of asset return, PA-MS-DR significantly outperforms baseline models in four of five datasets. MS-DR model is only slightly worse than PA-MS-DR. Under the normal distribution assumption, PA-MS-DR again outperforms baseline models with MS-DR behaving similarly as in the previous case. The improvement in performance can be ascribed to that our method utilized r^3 and r^4 as feature, which is associated with skewness and kurtosis of the asset. The dynamics of these higher order momentum information can be captured by the GRU module. Methods that assumes t-distribution of asset return performs better than methods that assumes normal distribution in stock market indexes data, while the reverse is true in foreign exchange rate data. This is consistent with previous studies [7,9].

In additional to the negative log-likelihood, we also conducted the Christophersen's independence test [6] and Kupiec's proportion of failures coverage test [15] on the predicted values. The result is also shown in Table 2.

The 0.05 quantile violation ratio result of Table 2 is listed separately in Table 3 to avoid confusion. It should be noted that, higher quantile violation ratio doesn't necessarily means a worse prediction. For the 0.05 quantile break experiment, the ideal quantile break ratio should be around 0.05.

Table 2. The negative log-likelihood of the test sets of stock indexes S&P 500, NAS-DAQ 100 and Nikkei 225 as well as exchange rate EUR-USD and JPY-USD. The result is the mean of the negative log-likelihood for 5 future days. suffix-t indicate using t-distribution. The bolded letters indicate the lowest value. i.e. the best result. The threshold for rejecting the null hypothesis with 90% confidence level is 2.7060 for Christophersen's independence test. $\star$ represents the threshold is exceeded. The threshold for rejecting the null hypothesis with 95% confidence level is 3.8415 for Kupiec's proportion of failures coverage test. † sign indicates the threshold is exceeded.

	S&P 500	NASDAQ 100	Nikkei 225	EUR-USD	JPY-USD
AR-GJR-GARCH-t	1.3819†	1.6078 †	1.5634	0.6020	0.5212†
GJR-GARCH-t	1.3711	1.6033†	1.5599	0.6038	0.5176†
GARCH-t	1.3668	1.6052†	1.5609	0.6046	0.5183†
PA-MS-DR-t	**1.2165**	**1.4924**	**1.5057†**	**0.6008$\star$**	**0.4950†**
MS-DR-t	1.2209	1.4971	1.5223†	0.6094	0.4983†
AR-GJR-GARCH	1.5318$\star$	1.6838†	1.6152	0.5897	0.4818$\star$†
GJR-GARCH	1.5058$\star$	1.6805†	1.5979	0.5925$\star$	0.4839
GARCH	1.5086$\star$	1.6682†	1.6050	**0.5924$\star$**	0.4840
PA-MS-DR	**1.2504$\star$**	**1.5360**	**1.5189†**	0.6023	**0.4604†**
MS-DR	1.2564 †	1.5611	1.5403	0.6099	0.4740†

Table 3. The quantile violation ratios. Kupiec's proportion of failures coverage test gives lower bond and upper bond of 0.0203 and 0.0813 for S&P 500, NASDAQ 100 and Nikkei 225 data, for EUR-USD and JPY-USD, the upper bond and lower bonds are 0.0182 and 0.0818

	S&P 500	NASDAQ 100	Nikkei 225	EUR-USD	JPY-USD
AR-GJR-GARCH-t	0.0182	0.0091	0.0211	0.0244	0.0149
AR-GARCH-t	0.0182	0.0091	0.0211	0.0252	0.0158
GJR-GARCH-t	0.0309	0.0091	0.0236	0.0211	0.0124
GARCH-t	0.0291	0.0091	0.0236	0.0236	0.0116
PA-MS-DR-t	0.0256	0.0235	0.0181	0.0242	0.003
MS-DR-t	0.0182	0.0203	0.0328	0.0505	0.002
AR-GJR-GARCH	0.0364	0.02	0.0374	0.0309	0.0241
AR-GARCH	0.0355	0.0182	0.0366	0.0301	0.0232
GJR-GARCH	0.0345	0.0182	0.0333	0.0309	0.0232
GARCH	0.0355	0.0164	0.0341	0.0301	0.0232
PA-MS-DR	0.0246	0.0245	0.0198	0.0505	0.004
MS-DR	0.0246	0.0256	0.0172	0.04545	0.005

5 Conclusion

In summary, we propose a multi-step probability density function prediction framework called parsimonious autoregressive multi-step density regression (PA-MS-DR) that conduct recursive multi-step prediction of probability density function and can tackle the heavy-tail problem of financial time series. Our model uses GRU to extract information from past time-steps and predict the distribution parameters of the probability density function of financial asset returns multiple days ahead. The model converts the predicted probability density function into model input of next time-step, thus constitutes an autoregressive model. This autoregressive structure is highly parsimonious, involving no additional parameter. Experimental result on real-world data shows that our model significantly outperforms non-autoregressive baseline models under the condition of significantly fewer model parameters, which demonstrates the validity of the autoregressive structure. Our model support both t-distribution and normal distribution, thus is fitted to model both the stock market data and foreign exchange rates data. The structure of our model contains a nested RNN substructure, which slows down training. To accelerate the training process, we invent a novel approximate back-propagation-through-time algorithm specifically for the model and its convergence is mathematically proved.

References

1. Blunsom, P., Grefenstette, E., Kalchbrenner, N.: A convolutional neural network for modelling sentences. In: Proceedings of the 52nd Annual Meeting of the Association for Computational Linguistics (2014)
2. Bollerslev, T.: Generalized autoregressive conditional heteroskedasticity. J. Econ. **31**(3), 307–327 (1986)
3. Bradbury, J., Merity, S., Xiong, C., Socher, R.: Quasi-recurrent neural networks. arXiv preprint arXiv:1611.01576 (2016)
4. Carnero, M.A., Peña, D., Ruiz, E.: Persistence and kurtosis in garch and stochastic volatility models. J. Financ. Econ. **2**(2), 319–342 (2004)
5. Cho, K., et al.: Learning phrase representations using RNN encoder-decoder for statistical machine translation. In: Proceedings of the 2014 Conference on Empirical Methods in Natural Language Processing (EMNLP), pp. 1724–1734 (2014)
6. Christoffersen, P.F.: Evaluating interval forecasts. Int. Econ. Rev. **39**(4), 841–862 (2001)
7. Coppes, R.C.: Are exchange rate changes normally distributed? Econ. Lett. **47**(2), 117–121 (1995)
8. Dunson, D.B., Pillai, N., Park, J.H.: Bayesian density regression. J. Roy. Stat. Soc. Ser. B (Stat. Method.) **69**(2), 163–183 (2007)
9. Egan, W.J.: The distribution of s&p 500 index returns. Social Science Electronic Publishing (2007)
10. Engle, R.F., Manganelli, S.: CAViaR: conditional autoregressive value at risk by regression quantiles. J. Bus. Econ. Stat. **22**(4), 367–381 (2004)
11. Fleming, J., Kirby, C.: A closer look at the relation between garch and stochastic autoregressive volatility. J. Financ. Econ. **1**(3), 365–419 (2003)

12. Franses, P.H., Van Der Leij, M., Paap, R.: A simple test for garch against a stochastic volatility model. J. Financ. Econ. **6**(3), 291–306 (2007)
13. Glosten, L.R., Jagannathan, R., Runkle, D.E.: On the relation between the expected value and the volatility of the nominal excess return on stocks. J. Financ. **48**(5), 1779–1801 (1993)
14. Golub, G.H., Welsch, J.H.: Calculation of gauss quadrature rules. Math. Comput. **23**(106), 221–230 (1969)
15. Kupiec, P.H.: Techniques for verifying the accuracy of risk management models. Soc. Sci. Electron. Publishing **3**(2), 73–84 (1995)
16. Lei, T., Zhang, Y., Artzi, Y.: Training RNNs as fast as CNNs. arXiv preprint arXiv:1709.02755 (2017)
17. Mei, H., Eisner, J.M.: The neural hawkes process: a neurally self-modulating multivariate point process. In: Advances in Neural Information Processing Systems, pp. 6754–6764 (2017)
18. Shen, W., Ghosal, S., et al.: Adaptive bayesian density regression for high-dimensional data. Bernoulli **22**(1), 396–420 (2016)
19. Taylor, S.J.: Modeling stochastic volatility: a review and comparative study. Math. Financ. **4**(2), 183–204 (1994)
20. Venkatraman, A., Hebert, M., Bagnell, J.A.: Improving multi-step prediction of learned time series models. In: Twenty-Ninth AAAI Conference on Artificial Intelligence (2015)
21. Yan, X., Zhang, W., Ma, L., Liu, W., Wu, Q.: Parsimonious quantile regression of financial asset tail dynamics via sequential learning. In: Proceedings of Advances in Neural Information Processing Systems, vol. 31 (2018)

Big Data Financial Sentiment Analysis
in the European Bond Markets

Luca Tiozzo Pezzoli[✉], Sergio Consoli[✉], and Elisa Tosetti[✉]

JRC - European Commission, Ispra, Italy
{luca.tiozzo-pezzoli, sergio.consoli,
elisa.tosetti}@ec.europa.eu

Abstract. We exploit the novel Global Database of Events, Language and Tone (GDELT) to construct news-based financial sentiment measures capturing investor's opinions for three European countries, Italy, Spain and France. We study whether deterioration in investor's sentiment implies a rise in interest rates with respect to their German counterparts. Finally, we look at the link between agents' sentiment and their portfolio exposure on the Italian, French and Spanish markets.

Keywords: Government yield spread · Financial sentiment · Random forest · Quantile regression

1 Introduction

The recent surge in the government yield spreads in countries within the Euro area has originated an intense debate about the determinants and sources of risk of sovereign spreads. Traditionally, factors such as the creditworthiness, the sovereign bond liquidity risk, and general risk aversion have been identified as the main factors having an impact on government yield spreads (see, among others, Monfort and Renne (2011), Swartz (2019), Beber, Brandt and Kavajecz (2009)). However, a recent literature has pointed at the important role of financial investor's sentiment in determining and anticipating interest rates dynamics (Tetlock (2007) and Loughran and McDonald (2011)).

This paper exploits a novel, open source, news database known as Global Database of Events, Language and Tone dataset (GDELT) to construct news-based financial sentiment indicators related to economic and political events for a set of Euro area countries. We first study whether changes in the financial sentiment of both domestic and international investors as measured by our news-based sentiment indicators has an impact on government yield spreads, after controlling for a set of variables measuring economic and financial fundamentals. The aim is to evaluate how the dynamics of yield spread for one country are affected by the financial sentiment measured within the country as well the sentiment measured in other countries. In the last part of the paper we examine the link between the composition of banks' sovereign bond portfolios in the Eurozone and our measures of risks.

© Springer Nature Switzerland AG 2020
V. Bitetta et al. (Eds.): MIDAS 2019, LNAI 11985, pp. 122–126, 2020.
https://doi.org/10.1007/978-3-030-37720-5_10

2 Data and Methodology

GDELT is an open Big Data platform on news collected at worldwide level. It provides translation in over 65 languages, extracts people, locations, organizations, counts, quotes, images and millions of themes from commonly used practitioners' topical taxonomies, such as the World Bank Topical Taxonomy. It also measures thousands of emotional dimensions expressed by means of dictionaries popular in the literature, such as the IV-4 Harvard Psychosocial Dictionary or WordNet Affect. In terms of volume, GDELT analyses over 88 million articles a year and more than 150,000 news outlets. Its dimension is around 8 TB, growing 2 TB each year.

We extracted all news articles for which the main location is one of the three leading European countries, namely Italy, Spain and France, over the period from February 2015 until December 2018. Given that we wish to measure financial sentiment related to economic and political events (rather than events in general), we restricted our attention to articles for which the themes extracted by GDELT falls into one of the World Bank topics: Macroeconomic Vulnerability and Debt, Macroeconomic and Structural Policies, Financial Sector Development, Economic Growth. We measured the sentiment of news according with different dictionaries used by financial practitioners and provided by GDELT (such as the Loughran and McDonald (2011)). In a second step, we have applied the random forest approach on the extracted emotions, using, as outcome variables, the Italian, French and Spanish 10-year government bond yield spreads with respect to German benchmark. In the Random Forest approach, following existing literature, we controlled for financial indexes measuring credit risk, liquidity risk and risk aversion (see, among others, Beber, Brandt and Kavajecz (2009), Garcia and Gimeno (2014), Manganelli and Wolswijk (2009), Favero, Pagano and von Thadden (2010), Monfort and Renne (2011), Bernal, Gnabo and Guilmin (2016)), extracted from the Bloomberg data base. We have performed a 10-fold cross-validation and grid search for parameters estimation. Figure 1 shows the temporal evolution of the Italian spread versus two important sentiments selected via Random Forest approach, namely diffidence and gratefulness. The blue and the red shadows indicate political events that may have led to economic uncertainty, namely the difficulty to set up the new government in Italy (in red) and the French election (in blue). In these periods, the graph shows a clear increasing pattern for diffidence, and a decreasing pattern for gratefulness. Once selected our sentiment indicators, we have included these along with the financial indexes in a classical regression approach. We use a quantile regression method introduced by Koenker and Bassett (1978) that allows us to study the impact of our financial sentiment indexes to the entire yield spreads distribution.

Table 1 displays the quantile regression output for Italy. It is interesting to observe that our news-based financial sentiment indicators help to explain tail behaviour of yield spread distribution. In particular, results show that diffidence increases during political and economic uncertain periods and impacts positively the right tail. On the other hand, Gratefulness impacts positively the left tail.

In a final step, we analyse how investors' sentiment is related to financial portfolio decisions, by looking at the relationship between foreign investments and our sentiment indicators. Figure 2 shows the temporal evolution of foreign investments (in blue) against the time series of one of our selected features for Italy (Diffidence). From the graph it is interesting to see that when Diffidence grows foreign investors decrease. This pattern seems to indicate that political and economic events may deteriorate the confidence of investors, as measured by our sentiment indicators, and encourage them to leave Italy, looking for safer destinations. Finally, Fig. 3 highlights a negative correlation between investments and media diffidence in Italy. However, the level of frustration expressed in the financial news in France seems not to affect investments.

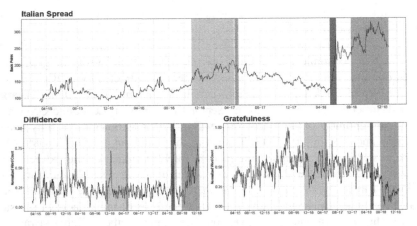

Fig. 1. The evolution of the Italian spread and financial sentiment (Color figure online)

Table 1. Quantile regression for Italy

	Dependent variable: $\Delta Spread_l^{IT}$				
	$q = 0.10$	$q = 0.30$	$q = 0.50$	$q = 0.70$	$q = 0.90$
Constant	−5.343***	−1.980***	0.037	−1.816***	5.760***
	(0.000)	(0.000)	(0.791)	(0.000)	(0.000)
CRD_l^{IT}	2.058***	1.751***	1.1851***	2.025***	2.996***
	(0.000)	(0.000)	(0 000)	(0 000)	(0.000)
ΔLIQ_l^{IT}	0.014	0.642	0.520	0 518	0.762
	(0.983)	(0.184)	(0.196)	(0.372)	(0.517)
$\Delta RAVE_l^{IT}$	−0.206	−0.124	−0.146	−0.245	−0.480
	(0.334)	(0.251)	(0.232)	(0.122)	(0.141)
$GDELT_{Diff,l}^{IT}$	−0.538*	−0.016	0.042	0.440*	1.389***
	(0.095)	(0.938)	(0.801)	(0.064)	(0.004)
$GDELT_{Grale,l}^{IT}$	0.914***	0.302***	0.079	−0.071	−0.443
	(0.000)	(0.010)	(0.559)	(0.685)	(0.159)
R_{nested}^2	0.15	0.12	0.12	0.12	0.19
R^2	0.18	0.12	0.12	0.12	0.21
	(0.00)	(0.03)	(0.83)	(0.15)	(0.01)

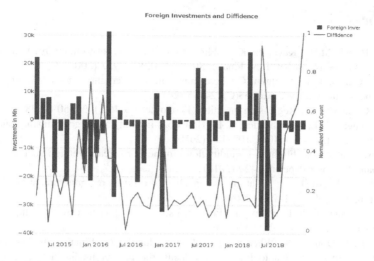

Fig. 2. The relation between financial investments and investors diffidence (Color figure online)

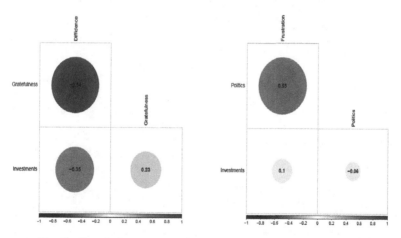

Fig. 3. Correlation measures between sentiments and investments

Our analysis is one of the first to study the behaviour of government yield spreads and financial portfolio decisions in the presence of liquidity, credit and financial sentiment measures. We believe our financial sentiment measures are able to capture and predict changes in interest rates dynamics in a more timely manner.

References

Beber, A., Brandt, M.W., Kavajecz, K.A.: Flight-to-quality or flight-to-liquidity? Evidence from the Euro-area bond market. Rev. Financ. Stud. **22**(3), 925–957 (2009)

Bernal, O., Gnabo, J.-Y., Guilmin, G.: Economic policy uncertainty and risk spillover in the Eurozone. J. Int. Money Finan. **65**(C), 24–45 (2016)

Koenker, R., Bassett, G.: Regression quantiles. Econometrica **46**(1), 33–50 (1978)

Favero, C., Pagano, M., von Thadden, E.-L.: How does liquidity affect government bond yields? J. Financ. Quant. Anal. **45**(01), 107–134 (2010)

Garcia, J.A., Gimeno, R.: Flight-to-Liquidity flows in the Euro area sovereign debt crisis. Banco de Espana Working Paper n. 1429 (2014)

Manganelli, S., Wolswijk, G.: What drives spreads in the Euro area government bond market? Econ. Policy **24**(58), 191–240 (2009)

Monfort, A., Renne, J.-P.: Decomposing Euro-area sovereign spreads: credit and liquidity risks. Rev. Finance **18**(6), 2103–2151 (2011)

Loughran, T., McDonald, B.: When is a liability not a liability? J. Finance **66**, 35–65 (2011)

Tetlock, P.C.: Giving content to investor sentiment: the role of media in the stock market. J. Finance **3**, 1139–1168 (2007)

Schwartz, K.: Mind the gap: disentangling credit and liquidity in risk spreads. Rev. Finance **23**(3), 557–597 (2019)

A Brand Scoring System
for Cryptocurrencies Based
on Social Media Data

Giuseppe Santomauro[1]([⊠]), Daniela Alderuccio[2], Fiorenzo Ambrosino[1],
Andrea Fronzetti Colladon[4], and Silvio Migliori[3]

[1] ENEA - C.R. Portici, DTE-ICT-HPC, P.le E. Fermi, 1, 80055 Portici, NA, Italy
{giuseppe.santomauro,fiorenzo.ambrosino}@enea.it
[2] ENEA - Sede Legale, DTE-ICT-HPC, L. Thaon di Revel, 76, 00196 Rome, Italy
daniela.alderuccio@enea.it
[3] ENEA - Sede Legale, DTE-ICT, L. Thaon di Revel, 76, 00196 Rome, Italy
silvio.migliori@enea.it
[4] Department of Engineering, University of Perugia, Via G. Duranti, 93,
06125 Perugia, Italy
andrea.fronzetticolladon@unipg.it

Abstract. In this work, we present an overview on the development
and integration in ENEAGRID of some tools to evaluate brand importance of homogeneous financial instruments, such as cryptocurrencies.
Our system is based on the analysis of textual data, such as tweets or
online news. A collaborative environment called *Web Crawling* Virtual
Laboratory allows data retrieval from the web. Below we describe this
virtual lab and the ongoing activity aimed at adding a new feature, to
allow news and social media crawling. We also provide some details about
the integration in ENEAGRID of a new measure of brand importance
and its Virtual Laboratory, namely the *Semantic Brand Score*. We aim
to test the first version of this new virtual environment on *Twitter* data,
to rank digital currencies.

Keywords: Social network crawling · Semantic brand scoring ·
Cryptocurrency · Financial trends

1 Introduction

Cryptocurrencies are digital assets that are designed to work as the economic
component of a distributed ledger technology system such as a *blockchain*. They
use cryptography to manage several functionalities, as the secure exchange of
value between users or the creation of economic supply, over a distributed network, without having to trust central authorities.

The first and most popular cryptocurrency is *Bitcoin* [6]. It was released
in 2009; since then more than 3000 new digital coins have been created each of
them coming from a different project and having functionalities, from the simple
exchange of value to, for example, smart contracts.

© Springer Nature Switzerland AG 2020
V. Bitetta et al. (Eds.): MIDAS 2019, LNAI 11985, pp. 127–132, 2020.
https://doi.org/10.1007/978-3-030-37720-5_11

Units of these digital assets, sometimes also called *tokens*, are used for the economic incentive mechanism that motivate the different players of the distributed system. This tokens therefore have economic values and are exchangeable on the network itself. This has contributed to the arise of several marketplaces where users interact in trading activities with prices typically depending on demand and supply.

The demand of a token, hence its price, also depends on the quality and uniqueness of the underling service, or at least the way it is perceived. Characteristics include: the number of developers of the platform, who are the long-term investors and the size of the userbase.

The numerosity of users of a platform and their sentiment about the project can generate positive network effects facilitating the involvement of new users. To study these effects we propose to explore the Web (news, forums, tweets, etc.) and analyse messages users share about some cryptocurrencies. In order to compute a rank of cryptocurrencies based on their relevance, we consider a method that extracts important information from the Web, concerning the topic of digital coins and to applies a semantic algorithm that elaborates a score.

The task of downloading a large amount of data from the Internet, that is the World's largest data source, is commonly known as *Web Crawling*. In this context, the task of performing a brand ranking from a large set of text data (news, tweets, etc.) is named *Brand Scoring*. Both operations are critical points in terms of computational costs. For this reason, the advanced computing center of ENEA Portici, hosting the ENEAGRID/CRESCO infrastructure [8] is used to perform these activities.

In the following, we introduce the *Web Crawling* and the *Semantic Brand Score* virtual labs integrated in ENEAGRID, used to retrieve and analyze data from the Web. Finally, we provide details on a work-in-progress activity describing how to obtain financial news from social networks and how to compute a rank of brand awareness for digital coins.

2   Web Crawling in ENEAGRID

Generally, a crawling technique searches for documents to download by systematically and automatically analyzing the content of a network. A web crawler starts from a list of URLs to visit. When it downloads a web page then it updates this list by new URLs retrieved by parsing the explored document. This process can be infinitely repeated and it can be stopped either when it reaches a target number of pages or after a fixed amount of time. In the next, we provide a description of our web crawling environment installed on ENEAGRID.

2.1   The Software Solution

As software solution, we decided to integrate the *BUbiNG* [2] program into ENEAGRID. It is an open source product that allows the parallel execution of multiple crawling agents. Each agent communicates with the others to ensure not repeated visits the same webpages and to balance computational load. *BUbiNG* also is able to save space up to around 80% by storing contents in compressed *warc.gz* files.

We did some tests to evaluate the performance of our software solution. We checked its efficiency, robustness and reliability by performing long-time and periodic crawling sessions: we obtained good results [9].

2.2   The Virtual Laboratory

We created a collaborative *Web Crawling Project* integrated in ENEAGRID. Here, the main issue consisted in harmonizing the tool in a typical HPC environment to exploit infrastructure resources, that are computational nodes, networking, storage systems, and job scheduler. All the web crawling instruments are combined in an ENEAGRID virtual laboratory, named *Web Crawling*. The virtual lab has a public web site[1] (Fig. 1(a)) where information about the research activity is collected, and a web application (Fig. 1(b)) with analytical tools and the display and clustering of web data.

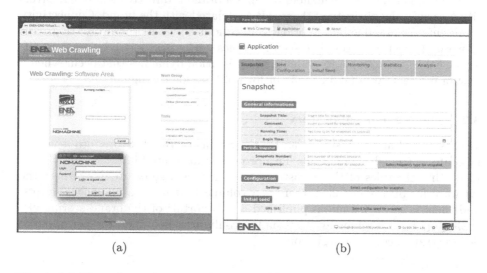

(a)   (b)

Fig. 1. (a) The web crawling virtual lab site. (b) The web crawling virtual lab GUI.

3   Semantic Brand Scoring in ENEAGRID

The *Semantic Brand Score* (SBS) is a novel metric designed to assess the importance of one or more brands, in different contexts and whenever it is possible to analyze textual data, even big data [3]. The advantage with respect to some traditional measures is that the SBS do not relies on surveys administered to small samples of consumers.

---

[1] http://www.afs.enea.it/project/webcrawl/.

3.1   The Metric

The measure can be calculated on any source of text documents, such as newspaper articles, emails, tweets, posts on online forums, blogs and social media. The idea is to capture insights coming from honest signals [7], through the analysis of big textual data and combining methods of text mining and social network analysis. Spontaneous expressions of consumers, or other brand stakeholders, can be collected from the places where they normally appear—for example a travel forum, if studying the importance of museum brands. This has the advantage of reducing the biases induced by the use of questionnaires, where interviewees know that they are being observed. The SBS can also be adapted to different languages and to study the importance of specific words, or set of words, not necessarily *brands* [3]. The SBS measures brand importance, which is at the basis of brand equity [3]. Indeed the metric was partially inspired by well-known conceptualizations of brand equity and by the constructs of brand image and brand awareness [1,5]. Brand importance is measured along the three dimensions of prevalence, diversity and connectivity. Prevalence measures the frequency of use of the brand name, i.e. the number of times a brand is directly mentioned. Diversity measures the diversity of the words associated with the brand. Connectivity represents the brand ability to bridge connections between other words or groups of words (sometimes seen as discourse topics). The SBS has been used in different fields, for example to evaluate the transition dynamics that occur when a new brand replaces an old one [3], or for political forecasting [4].

3.2   The Virtual Laboratory

We assembled all the instruments for the Semantic Brand Score into a virtual laboratory, named *Brand Score*. This project is integrated into ENEAGRID by respecting the rules of the infrastructure. There is a software area, where the software for SBS is installed; there is a volume that holds all launcher scripts; and there is an area where is published a web portal[2] of the brand scoring virtual lab (Fig. 2). Preliminary tests on the configuration and on the performance demonstrate a correct integration.

4   Proposal of Current Development

We are currently working to an extension of our web crawling tool to retrieve data from social media, in order to discover news and discussions on a specific financial topic, such as digital coins, and to calculate the Semantic Brand Score.

4.1   Social Networks Crawling

In recent years, news on politics, sport and the economy have grown considerably on social media. For this reason, we decided to extend the features of our tools

---

[2] http://www.afs.enea.it/project/brandscore/.

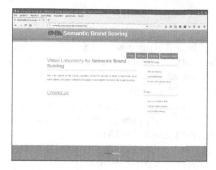

Fig. 2. The semantic brand score virtual lab site.

with a social media crawler. We are currently equipping our environment with a *Twitter* crawler. The software solution that we adopted is based on the *JAVA* language. By considering the *Twitter* access rules that limit the number of tweets downloaded per user and by exploiting the APIs of this social network, we created manifold developer accounts. In this way, we can launch parallel sessions of the *JAVA* software (agents) on a specific topic or on a set of themes. We can collect the *tweets* in JSONs files indexed for *hashtag* and for downloading timestamp. Preliminary tests confirm a good performance in terms of number of tweets per time unit.

4.2 Semantic Brand Score and Cryptocurrencies

Once the configuration of the *Twitter* crawler will be fully optimized, we are plan running periodic sessions of crawling in order to create a database of tweets that concern news and discussions about digital coins. This data will be analyzed through the Semantic Brand Score, to rank cryptocurrency importances.

5   Conclusions

To summarize, we provided an overview of activity about the implementation of a social media crawler that downloads contents from *Twitter*. The tool is integrated in our HPC ENEAGRID/CRESCO infrastructure. Currently we are also equipping our framework with a semantic brand scoring tool which uses ENEA computational and storage power. First tests on the social crawler and on the SBS software demonstrate good results.

Acknowledgements. The computing resources and the related technical support used for this work have been provided by ENEAGRID/CRESCO High Performance Computing infrastructure and its staff [8]. ENEAGRID/CRESCO High Performance Computing infrastructure is funded by ENEA, the Italian National Agency for New Technologies, Energy and Sustainable Economic Development and by Italian and European research programmes, see http://www.cresco.enea.it/english for information.

References

1. Aaker, D.A.: Measuring brand equity across products and markets. Calif. Manag. Rev. **38**, 102–120 (1996). https://doi.org/10.2307/41165845
2. Boldi, P., Marino, A., Santini, M., Vigna, S.: BUbiNG: massive crawling for the masses. CoRR abs/1601.06919 (2016)
3. Fronzetti Colladon, A.: The semantic brand score. J. Bus. Res. **88**, 150 – 160 (2018). https://doi.org/10.1016/j.jbusres.2018.03.026, http://www.sciencedirect.com/science/article/pii/S0148296318301541
4. Fronzetti Colladon, A.: Forecasting election results by studying brand importance in online news. Int. J. Forecast. (2019, in press)
5. Keller, K.L.: Conceptualizing, measuring, and managing customer-based brand equity. J. Mark. **57**(1), 1–22 (1993). http://www.jstor.org/stable/1252054
6. Nakamoto, S.: Bitcoin: a peer-to-peer electronic cash system, December 2008. https://bitcoin.org/bitcoin.pdf. Accessed 01 June 2019
7. Pentland, A.S.: Honest Signals: How They Shape Our World. The MIT Press, Cambridge (2010)
8. Ponti, G., et al.: The role of medium size facilities in the HPC ecosystem: the case of the new CRESCO4 cluster integrated in the ENEAGRID infrastructure, pp. 1030–1033 (2014)
9. Santomauro, G., et al.: A collaborative environment for web crawling and web data analysis in ENEAGRID. In: DATA 2017, Madrid, Spain, 24–26 July 2017, pp. 287–295 (2017)

Author Index

Printed in the United States
By Bookmasters